Praise for the Previous Edition

"If you hanker after a slice of the good life, like to know the provenance of your food or simply want to be thrifty, this . . . is an excellent place to start."
—*Food and Travel Magazine*

"A comprehensive look at all aspects of turning home-grown produce into delicious treats."
—*Country Kitchen*

"What I loved about this book was discovering new things to do with vegetables that I hadn't thought of before . . . This is a handy book to keep in your cupboard for autumn harvest and the excess fruit and vegetables that come your way."
—*The Rural*

"A little gem of a book."
—*Highland Life*

© 2024 by Carol Wilson and IMM Lifestyle Books, an imprint of Fox Chapel Publishing Company, Inc.

Portions of *Guide to Canning and Preserving Food* (2024) are taken from *Self-Sufficiency: Preserving* (2016), published by IMM Lifestyle Books, an imprint of Fox Chapel Publishing Company, Inc.

Portions of *Guide to Canning and Preserving Food* (2024) are taken from *Amish Community Cookbook* (2017), published by Fox Chapel Publishing Company, Inc.

ISBN 978-1-5048-0142-3

The Cataloging-in-Publication Data is on file with the Library of Congress.

To learn more about the other great books from Fox Chapel Publishing, or to find a retailer near you, call toll-free 800-457-9112, send mail to 903 Square Street, Mount Joy, PA 17552, or visit us at *www.FoxChapelPublishing.com*.

We are always looking for talented authors. To submit an idea, please send a brief inquiry to acquisitions@foxchapelpublishing.com.

Printed in China
First printing

This book has been published with the intent to provide accurate and authoritative information in regard to the subject matter within. While every precaution has been taken in the preparation of this book, the author and publisher expressly disclaim any responsibility for any errors, omissions, or adverse effects arising from the use or application of the information contained herein.

GUIDE TO
CANNING AND
PRESERVING FOOD

Easy Recipes and Tips for Making Jams, Jellies, Chutneys, Pickles, and More

Carol Wilson

IMM
lifestylebooks™
Read. Learn. Do What You Love.

Table of Contents

Fill your pantry with homemade preserves that taste better than what you buy at the store.

Introduction

There's something very satisfying about opening a cupboard and surveying splendid rows of gleaming glass jars filled with homemade jams, jellies, chutneys, pickles, and bottled fruits. It always gives me a warm glow of achievement to know that all these delicious preserves are homemade from garden produce—if not my own, then from a local farmer or vendor at a farmers market.

Preserving fruits and vegetables is one of the oldest culinary traditions. Fruit preserves have a long history—the ancient Greeks used to preserve quinces by packing them into jars filled with honey and storing them until the fruit was soft. The arrival of sugar in Europe caused a revolution in the kitchen, and by the 17th century, it was more readily available and affordable, and preserving fruits with sugar became very fashionable.

Preserving vegetables with salt or vinegar has also been practiced since ancient times. Pickles were enjoyed in antiquity: Julius Caesar was reputed to have been very fond of pickles, and Samuel Pepys mentions enjoying pickled "girkins" in his famous diary. Pickled gherkins and cucumbers started to be made in the 16th century in Germany and are still

enormously popular there as is sauerkraut (salted fermented cabbage).

All types of preserves were originally made to preserve fruits and vegetables from an all too fleeting summer and autumn, ready for consumption during the cold, harsh winter months. A good harvest could produce an abundance of fruits and vegetables—too many to be eaten immediately. In the days before refrigeration, these needed to be preserved before they spoiled.

Fermented foods are a rich source of vitamins and minerals as the process of fermentation increases the amount of certain vitamins.

Different methods of preserving were created to prevent food from decaying and to enable its consumption out of season; but as time passed, preserved foods became popular foods in their own right: sweet jams and jellies provided deliciously fruity spreads for plain bread and cakes, bottled fruits kept their shape and color and could be enjoyed all year round, pickled and salted foods enhanced the taste of bland meals, and all could be enjoyed out of season. We still enjoy preserves today—who can resist a spoonful of fragrant homemade strawberry jam to brighten up simple toast with butter, or a helping of piquant chutney or pickles to liven up a cheese board?

Previous generations had to preserve the culinary riches of summer and autumn for the bleak winter months out of necessity. Country housewives collected produce from gardens, hedgerows, woods, and fields and preserved them with sugar, salt, or vinegar. Some, such as bottled gooseberries and quince paste, were treasured as delicacies and kept until Christmas to enjoy as a special treat.

The advent of refrigerators and freezers meant that people no longer had to rely on the old methods, and the art of preserving was sadly almost lost for a while. Thankfully, self-sufficiency is back in vogue, partly from a desire for high-quality foods with that inimitable real homemade taste, and partly from a wish to find alternatives sources away from the grocery store. It is important that these skills are not lost, but making your own preserves is not only enjoyable but will also save you money.

In our great-grandmothers' day, it was considered the norm for families to go out to gather fruits and vegetables in season to get ready for "putting up preserves" in marathon cooking sessions. Nowadays, thanks to modern kitchens and equipment, it is quicker and easier than ever to make tasty preserves.

Backyards, community gardens, stores, and the countryside all provide an abundance of produce in season, and conserving a glut of seasonal produce is a time-honored method of filling the pantry. Whether your produce is homegrown, gathered from the wild, or bought from a shop (to take advantage of a seasonal abundance being sold cheaply), finding a ready supply of produce has never been easier.

Homemade preserves make great presents and are much appreciated by the recipient. They are always popular at food fairs and markets and are a wonderful way of raising money for charity fundraisers. I've always enjoyed making preserves for friends and family, who love to receive them as gifts. There's a particular pleasure in giving something you've made yourself, and of course, they taste so much better than large-scale commercial versions, which are often horribly oversweet or crammed with additives. What could be better than a shimmering amethyst blackberry jam made from freshly picked, sun-ripened berries, or tangy pickled vegetables?

The preserving methods in this book are clearly explained and paired with details of the equipment needed, information on ingredients, cooking techniques, and storage instructions. Each tried-and-tested recipe is clear and easy to follow with step-by-step instructions. Plus, there is a section for each chapter on what can go wrong—usually this happens if a recipe isn't followed correctly or the preserves are incorrectly stored.

You'll find some old favorites as well as new and unusual preserves that will please you, your family, and friends. And of course, they have the added appeal of being made with love and care.

Preserved food comes in a wide variety of techniques and styles.

Preserving

There are several different methods of preserving fruits and vegetables and all give delicious results. Jams, jellies, fruit butters and curds, bottled fruits, chutneys, pickles, salted vegetables, and dried fruit and vegetables are all practical and economical ways to preserve seasonal produce.

TYPES OF PRESERVE

- **Jam** is a thick mixture of fruit and sugar, cooked until the pieces of fruit are very soft and almost formless. Fruit jams were originally regarded as luxury foods and saved for celebrations and holidays.
- **Jelly** is a translucent mixture made from fruit juice, sugar, and sometimes pectin. It should be brilliantly clear, and the texture should wobble but still hold its shape.
- **Marmalade** was originally a medieval confection made from quinces. Marmalades made from other fruits, such as cherries and plums, appeared in the 17th century—although these marmalades would not be familiar to us today as they were firm enough to slice and were eaten as a dessert. As time passed, only citrus fruits were used to make marmalade. The first orange marmalade was made from bitter Seville oranges.
- **Fruit butter and curd** don't necessarily contain butter; the name refers to their velvety, almost creamy texture, which is stiffer and smoother than that of jam. Fruit butters are soft and spreadable, while curds are thicker. Both have

only a short shelf life as they don't contain as much sugar in proportion to fruit as jam, so they are usually made in small quantities and stored in the refrigerator.

- **Chutney** is a sweet-spicy relish made with sugar and vinegar. It originated in India (the name comes from *chatni*, meaning "a strong, sweet relish") and first appeared in Europe in the 17th century, when it became very popular for pepping up bland foods. Chutney is cooked slowly to produce a rich, full flavor and may be very hot and spicy or mild and aromatic, depending on the ingredients used.

- **Pickles** are a time-honored method of preserving vegetables in a brine or vinegar mixture and may be sour, sweet, hot, or mild. The English word "pickle" is derived from the medieval word *pikel*, which meant "a spicy sauce served with meat or fowl." It's also related to the Middle Dutch word *pekel*, meaning "a solution (usually spiced brine) for preserving and flavoring food." Vinegar is a powerful preservative as few bacteria can survive in its acidic environment. The vegetables stay crisp and develop a tangy flavor. Cucumbers are the most-commonly pickled vegetables in Eastern Europe, often with spices, herbs, and sometimes a few oak or cherry leaves for extra flavor.

- **Fermented foods** are a rich source of vitamins and minerals as the process of fermentation increases the amounts of certain vitamins; sauerkraut, for instance, is a very good source of vitamin C. It was often included in military rations in ancient armies and was used to prevent scurvy.

- **Bottling fruit** is a practice that dates to antiquity. The ancient Romans filled jars with fruits and covered them with juice, wine, vinegar, or honey, then sealed the jars to make them airtight. Nowadays, bottled fruits are prepared by sterilizing the fruit in large wide-necked jars so the fruit stays whole. Any fruit can be bottled, including fruits like peaches and tomatoes, which can't be preserved by freezing. Bottled fruit keep indefinitely and are ready to serve as soon as they are made. As the fruit remains whole, bottled fruit is usually eaten as a dessert with cream, on ice cream or custard, in trifle, etc.

- **Salting vegetables** is an ancient method of preservation and is excellent for preserving runner and French beans in particular, which have a completely different flavor from canned or frozen beans. In Eastern Europe, salting vegetables and even some fruits are a common practice. Salted white cabbage (sauerkraut) is left until it has fermented and is particularly popular in Germany and Eastern Europe.

- **Drying** is one of the oldest methods of preserving. It removes the water from fruits and vegetables and so deactivates the harmful microbes that cause spoiling. Thus, the foods are preserved for a long time. Drying foods also concentrates their flavor. Use top-quality fruits and vegetables that are unblemished. The moisture content of each item and the thickness of the slices will affect drying time, so the timings given in this book are only approximate.

All these methods are both practical and economical ways of preserving seasonal produce.

Jams, Jellies, and Marmalades

These jewel-colored fruit preserves have been popular for hundreds of years and are an economical way of using up surplus fruit. Jams, jellies, and marmalades are wonderful for preserving the flavors of luscious seasonal fruits to enjoy all year. They are delicious as a spread for bread, as a filling for tarts and sponge cakes, and melted as a dessert sauce for ice cream.

Jams, jellies, and marmalades allow for seasonal goodness year-round.

A good wooden spoon and sturdy glass jars make all the difference.

Equipment

There are a few tools you need for making jams and jellies. I will mention when a tool is optional or provide alternatives if possible. Don't use the same equipment for vinegar preserves when making jam as cross contamination will spoil the flavor of the jam.

- Use **a large, deep, heavy-based pan** with plenty of room for the mixture to boil rapidly without boiling over. Special preserving pans are available, which are wider at the top with sloping sides to aid evaporation and ensure setting point is reached more quickly. It's worth investing in a preserving pan if you intend to make a lot of preserves.

- **A sturdy wooden spoon** with a long handle is best to ensure your hands are not too close to a boiling mixture when stirring. Consider using a slotted spoon to easily separate foam from the top or remove larger pieces.

- **A sugar/preserving thermometer** is useful, but not essential, to test that the correct temperature for setting point has been reached.

- For jelly making, you will need **a jelly bag** (from cookware shops). It should be scalded first—by pouring boiling water through it—so that the fruit juices don't soak into it.
- **A sieve** will separate the seeds from your jam, should you prefer a smoother texture. You will need to run your fruit mixture through the sieve before it's too thick, then it will return to the pot and cook the rest of the way.
- For marmalade making, **a potato peeler or zester** is helpful. Removing the rind and pith from citrus fruits is made a lot easier with this simple tool.
- **A wide funnel** is helpful when filling the jars, but a jug or a small ladle can be used instead.
- **Kilner® or Mason jars** are ideal for storing homemade preserves and come in a range of sizes. A Kilner jar is a glass jar that has a lid in two sections to ensure an airtight seal. A metal disc sits on top of the jar, and it is secured in place with a metal screw band containing a rubber seal. Another widely available glass jar has a rubber seal and a metal hinge, which forms an airtight seal when closed.
- **Wax discs and transparent cellophane covers** are an alternate to buying specialty jars that have a built-in seal. You can buy special packs containing glass jars, lids, and something to protect the preserves. Waxed circles are placed wax side down on top of the potted preserve, while still hot, to exclude air and prevent deterioration. Cellophane covers are dampened and placed on top of the potted preserve, when it is completely cold, then secured with an elastic band. The cellophane shrinks as it dries to form a tight seal over the jar. Elastic bands come in varying sizes from cookware and kitchen shops.

STERILIZING JARS

To allow for shrinkage, jars must be scrupulously cleaned and warmed before being filled to the brim. Wash the jars in hot soapy water, rinse very well, and put in a low oven for 15–20 minutes until warm and completely dry. Sterilize the lids in boiling water for 10 minutes, keeping them in the hot water until ready for use, then dry thoroughly with paper towels. An old country method to discourage mold from forming in stored jams was to brush the surface of the jar lids or the waxed discs with brandy before placing them over the hot jam.

Ingredients

Fruit for jams and jellies must be completely dry, firm, fresh, and ripe or slightly underripe. Don't use overripe produce as this may cause the finished preserve to ferment during storage. There's no need to remove pits that are difficult to dislodge from fruit—when the jam is boiling, the pits will float to the top and can be taken out then.

When making jam, fruit is prepared according to type. When making jelly, there's no need to do this as the fruit is strained in a jelly bag and the seeds, cores, skins, etc. are left in the jelly bag during the straining process.

Freshly picked blueberries taste better than store-bought.

POPULAR FRUITS FOR JAMS AND JELLIES

- **Apples** come in all shades of reds, greens, and yellows. They may be sweet, tart, soft and smooth, or crisp and crunchy, depending on the variety. Cooking apples are larger and have a sharper flavor than eating apples.
- **Apricots** have fragrant juicy flesh with a large kernel in the center that can be removed easily if the fruit is ripe.
- **Blackberries** are best when plump, ripe, and full of juice. Cultivated blackberries lack the deep flavor of wild berries, but they are still delicious and have the advantage of having fewer seeds than the wild variety.
- **Blackcurrants** have a rich, strong, sharp flavor and the dark purple berries are very popular for making into jam.
- **Blueberries**, also known as whortleberries or huckleberries, have a slight dusty bloom and tart flavor. They should be ripe but firm.
- **Cherries** may be almost black, bright red, pale pink, or yellow in color. It's best to taste them

before buying to check if they're sweet enough for your taste.
- **Elderberries** are the purple-black fruit of the elder tree. They must never be eaten raw and are always cooked.
- **Gooseberries** may be green, yellow, or red, although the sour green berries are the best for cooking.
- **Mulberries** are similar to blackberries but are more elongated and may be white, red, or black. They have a mild sweet flavor and make excellent jams.
- **Peaches**, when ripe, have a fragrant odor. The velvety skin may be red, blushed pink, yellow, or white. One side of the fruit has a distinctive vertical indentation.
- **Pears** have fine, soft, juicy flesh that, unusually, improves in both flavor and texture after they're picked. The skin may be bronze, green, pink, or red.
- **Plums** may be blue, green, purple, red, or yellow. The flesh is thick and juicy, and the flavor ranges from sweet to tart. **Damsons** are

a variety of plum, much smaller than cultivated plums, with a tart, strong flavor. When cooked, their flavor has a faint hint of almonds with a touch of spice. Damsons are indigestible when raw, but the sharp-tasting fruit is transformed during cooking and makes wonderful preserves. **Greengages** have a tender green-yellow or golden skin. The translucent golden flesh has an exquisitely sweet flavor, and it is regarded as one of the finest dessert plums. Victoria plums have yellow- to rose-colored skins, and their pink-hued flesh is rich, sweet, and juicy when ripe. Before the fruit is fully ripe, it is particularly good for making preserves.

- **Quinces** are exquisitely perfumed. Although hard and inedible when raw, they make delectable preserves. The fruit has a yellowish-green skin covered with down that is scrubbed off before use.

- **Raspberries** are sweet and fragrant with a velvety texture. Choose bright, firm berries, which may be red or yellow.

- **Rhubarb** is a vegetable but is often eaten as a fruit. "Forced" rhubarb (grown indoors in a dark location) has tender pink stems, which have a refreshingly tart flavor. There's no need to peel young rhubarb, just remove any stringy bits. When using outdoor grown rhubarb, choose red stems; if the stems are green, the flavor will be very sour and acid. It is important to note that rhubarb leaves are highly poisonous and must be discarded.

- **Strawberries** have a gloriously scented flavor and soft, luscious texture. Choose firm, plump, scarlet berries with very few green or white patches. Very large berries often lack flavor. Don't wash them until just before you want to use them. Rinse the fruits very gently, and hull the berries *after* washing to avoid making them soggy—the hull acts as a "plug."

Smaller, bright red strawberries usually have the best flavor.

ADDITIONAL INGREDIENTS

Sugar is the preserving agent, and granulated white sugar is fine. It is not essential to buy special preserving sugar; however, the larger crystals dissolve quickly, create less foam than ordinary sugar, and produce a clearer, more translucent jam. Preserving sugar is meant to be used with fruits high in pectin, such as gooseberries and blackcurrants. Jam sugar is granulated sugar with added pectin and is designed for fruits low in pectin, such as strawberries, cherries, and rhubarb. Superfine or brown sugar is not recommended (unless specifically stated in the ingredients) as these tend to produce a lot of foam.

Pectin, a natural gelling agent found in ripe fruit, helps jam and jelly to set. The amount of pectin present depends on the type of fruit and its ripeness. Some fruits, including apples, blackcurrants, and quinces have high levels of pectin. Others, such as cherries, elderberries, and strawberries, are low in pectin and must have additional pectin added for good results. In this case, lemon juice (which is naturally high in pectin), commercial liquid, or powdered pectin should be added, and this will be stated in the recipe.

OTHER TYPES OF SUGAR

- **Demerara:** large, sparkling golden crystals with a sticky, crunchy texture and light molasses flavor.
- **Light muscovado:** moist, fine-grained crystals with a rich aroma and glorious fudgy flavor.
- **Dark muscovado:** dark brown sugar with a sticky texture and rich toffee flavor.
- **Molasses:** the richest of all the sugars, with a distinctive deep, dark, treacly flavor.

Cooking

While many people don't understand the differences between jams, jellies, and marmalades, the true difference is in how they are prepared. There are important differences that distinguish each preserve. Jellies need to be strained before they are cooked to achieve their translucent luster while marmalades include citrus peels. Beyond that, the instructions are largely similar to making jams, so that section will be the most in depth.

JAMS

Lightly grease the inside of the pan with butter before you start making jam to reduce the amount of foam on the surface of a boiling mixture. The pan should never be more than half full to ensure sufficient space for rapid boiling after the sugar has been added. The fruit should simmer slowly at first to ensure that all the pectin is extracted. Cover the pan while the fruit is simmering.

Warm the sugar first by spreading it on a baking tray and placing in a low oven at 250°F (120°C/gas ½) for about 10 minutes. Add to the fruit and water so it dissolves more quickly.

The sugar is added when the fruit is soft. Whichever type of sugar you use, it should be allowed to dissolve completely before the mixture is brought to a boil. If the sugar is not dissolved completely when the mixture starts boiling, the preserve will be difficult to set and is likely to crystallize during storage. To test if the sugar is dissolved, dip a wooden spoon in the mixture, and if no sugar crystals are visible in the liquid that coats the back of the spoon, it has dissolved. Uncover the pan when the sugar has been added, and stir only occasionally to prevent sticking and burning.

The mixture should then boil steadily and rapidly to ensure setting point is reached in the shortest time. Don't stir the mixture continually while it is boiling as this will lower the temperature and delay the setting point.

A good set depends on the amounts of pectin, acid (naturally found in fruit), and sugar. Acid helps to release the pectin, which works with sugar to form a gel and set the jam. Some jams will reach setting point after just a few minutes boiling, while others will take 15 minutes or more.

To tell when setting point has been reached, remove the pan from the heat and put a teaspoon of a boiling mixture on a chilled saucer. As it cools, the jam will begin to set. It will wrinkle when pushed gently with your finger and will remain in two separate parts when you draw your finger through it. It is a good idea to prepare three or four saucers in the freezer or refrigerator for testing purposes.

If using a sugar thermometer, keep this in warm water until ready to use, so that the temperature of a boiling jam isn't reduced too much when you put it into the mixture.

Don't let the thermometer touch the base of the pan or you may get a false reading. Turn the thermometer around in the mixture to get an accurate reading. It should read 220°F (104°C).

> *Dull jam, jelly, or marmalade is due to cooking too long after adding the sugar.*

If setting point hasn't been reached, return to the heat and boil for a few minutes only before testing again. Don't overcook; if the mixture is boiled for too long, it won't set.

If using whole fruits, the recipe will state to let the hot jam stand for several minutes before pouring into jars. If the jam or jars are too hot, fruit will rise to the top, spoiling the appearance of the finished product. When setting point has been reached, remove the pan from the heat and let the mixture stand for about 10–15 minutes until a skin forms on the surface. Skim off any foam and stir once to distribute the fruit before pouring into the warmed jars. Alternatively, after removing the pan from the heat, stir in a small knob of butter (approximately two tablespoons) to disperse the foam.

To check if your jam has set, place a spoonful on a chilled plate. It will wrinkle when pushed with your finger.

Stand the warmed jars on folded newspaper or a wooden board to prevent cracking when the hot jam or jelly is poured in. Pour the mixture into the jars, filling them to the brim, as the jam will shrink a little as it cools. The less air space there is in the jars, the better the jam or jelly will keep.

Wipe the outside of the filled jars. If using, cover the surface of the hot jam with waxed circles, wax side down. If you forget to cover the jam with the discs while the jam is still hot, leave until completely cold—if the jam is covered while only warm, mold may grow on the surface.

Seal tightly with plastic lids, metal screw top lids, or wetted cellophane covers (wetted side up). Use elastic bands with the cellophane covers. Transparent cellophane covers will shrink as they dry to form a tight seal. Allow the jam to cool before applying the wetted cellophane covers. If these are applied before the jam is cooled, water can condense inside the covers, causing mold.

Finally, label with the name of the jam and the date. Store in a cool, dark, dry, and well-ventilated place. Some preserves tend to lose a little color if exposed to light. A warm, moist atmosphere will cause the jam to shrink, and dampness will encourage mold. Most jams will keep for up to a year. Once opened, store in the refrigerator.

JELLIES

Making jelly is almost identical to making jam, and the equipment is much the same. However, you will also need a jelly bag. This is made of heavy-duty cotton, muslin, or nylon with a very close weave. The bag must be scalded with boiling water before use to sterilize it and to avoid the fruit juices soaking into the bag.

Fruits high in pectin, such as blackcurrants, redcurrants, and gooseberries, are best for jelly making. Those with a low pectin content, such as blackberries or cherries, are best combined with a high-pectin fruit, such as redcurrants or apples, or made using sugar with pectin. There's no need to destone, hull, or core fruit for jellies as the cooked mixture is strained through a jelly bag. The fruit should be cooked slowly to extract the pectin.

Suspend the jelly bag from a hook or from the legs of an upturned stool or chair. Place a large bowl underneath to catch the juice. Ladle the fruit pulp and juices into the jelly bag, and leave to drip into the bowl for several hours or overnight. Don't

Juices will drip slowly though the jelly bag, but it will result in a clear and delicious preserve.

squeeze the bag to speed up the process or the jelly will be cloudy.

The juice is then boiled with sugar until setting point is reached—the amount of sugar needed depends on the type and weight of the fruits used and will be stated in the recipe. The cooking time can vary from 30 minutes to over an hour, according to the ripeness of the fruit. Because of the method used to extract the juice, it is difficult to estimate the final amount produced, so it is best to have more warmed jars ready than you think you will need. As a general guide, 5 cups or 2 lbs 3 oz (1 kg) sugar should make about five 8-oz (250 mL) jars or 3 lbs 5 oz (1.5 kg) jelly. Jellies are best potted as soon as possible; if left to stand, they start to gel in the pan.

The high temperature causes the pectin to react, so a boiling mixture must not be stirred, although you can skim off the foam that rises to the top as the mixture boils.

Jelly is potted in the same way as jam (page 18). Remove any foam from the top of the jelly with a metal spoon or stir slowly to disperse. To avoid air bubbles forming, tilt the jar and pour in the hot jelly slowly. Seal and label. Don't move the jars until the jelly has set completely. Once opened, store in the refrigerator.

MARMALADE

Marmalade is made in the same way as jam (page 17), but because it is made with citrus fruit, it needs a longer cooking time. The tough peel needs to be cooked until soft, so more water is needed. The same equipment is required for making marmalade as for jams and jellies, with the addition of a sharp knife and a juice extractor.

Bitter or Seville oranges, with their aromatic peel and intensely flavored astringent juice, are frequently used in marmalades. Use a zester or potato peeler to remove the rind. Don't include the white pith as this will give a bitter taste.

> *Don't include the white pith in your marmalade, as this will give a bitter taste.*

Lemons have a sharp citrus flavor. Choose thin-skinned fruits that are heavy for their size and bright yellow; those with a thicker peel will have less flesh and therefore be less juicy. Avoid any that are tinged with green as they're not fully ripe and will be very acidic. Use a potato peeler to remove the rind in thin strips and don't include the white pith.

Limes are oval or round in shape with green flesh and skin and are more fragrant than lemons. Choose limes that are firm and heavy for their size,

To make marmalade, put the pith and seeds into a piece of muslin. Wrap up like a bag, and put into the pot with the rinds. You need attach a piece of string to pull it out from the boiling water.

with deep green shiny skin. Use unwaxed fruits if possible.

Grapefruits are large citrus fruits with a refreshingly tart flavor and yellow or pink rind. They are available in both seeded and seedless varieties. Choose fruits that are heavy for their size, which indicates a good amount of juicy flesh, and sweet aroma.

Use unwaxed citrus fruits if possible; otherwise, the fruit must be well scrubbed under hot running water to remove the protective waxy coating or fungicide. Dry thoroughly. The peel may be cut finely or coarsely, according to preference. The pectin, which sets the marmalade, is mainly contained in the pith and seeds, so these must

not be discarded but tied loosely in a piece of muslin and added to the pan. The secret of good marmalade is fast boiling: test after 15 minutes, then every 5 minutes after that. Test for setting in the same way as for jam (page 18).

When setting point has been reached, remove the pan from the heat and let the mixture stand for about 10–20 minutes, when a skin will form on the surface. This prevents the peels from rising to the surface after potting. Stir once before pouring into the jars so the peel will be suspended evenly in the jelly.

Cover the marmalade with a waxed disc when hot, but seal with a cellophane cover or lid when cold to prevent condensation.

WHAT CAN GO WRONG?

- **Moldy or fermented** jam, jelly, or marmalade occurs if the preserve is potted while warm (instead of hot or cold); if the jars are unsterilized, insufficiently covered, or incompletely sealed; or if stored in a damp place. If there is just a thin layer of grayish-white mold on top of the jam or jelly, scrape it off completely and taste the preserve. If it tastes pleasant, then it can be eaten and should be stored in the refrigerator. If the mold is evident throughout the preserve, then it will be inedible and should be thrown away.

- **Crystallization** (small sugary crystals that form during storage) occurs if the sugar is not completely dissolved before boiling, if too much sugar is used for the proportion of fruit, or if the preserve is cooked for too long. As this can't be rectified, it is probably best to use the jam or jelly as a hot sauce.

> *Store in a cool, dark, dry, and ventilated place as preserves tend to lose a little color if exposed to light.*

- **Dull** jam, jelly, or marmalade is due to cooking too long after adding the sugar.

- **Bubbles** dispersed in jelly is due to leaving the jelly too long before potting, causing it to over-thicken and trapping bubbles of air. Foam that hasn't been removed before potting will also spoil the appearance of a jelly but won't affect the taste.

- **Cloudy** jelly is due to pressing or squeezing the jelly bag in an attempt to speed up the process while the juice is dripping through the bag.

- **Fruit pieces rising** in the jam are due to potting it too soon. The jam should be allowed to rest for the time stated in the recipe before transferring into jars.

- **Tough marmalade peel** is due to the peel not being sufficiently softened in the fruit juice before adding the sugar. This cannot be remedied once the marmalade is made, so check that the peel is very soft before adding the sugar.

- **Very dark and sticky** jam or marmalade means it was overcooked.

- **Stiff and rubbery** jam is caused by using wrong proportions—usually insufficient sugar and water for the quantity of fruit.

- **Jam shrinking** away from the sides of the jar is caused by boiling for too long or not creating an airtight seal when covering the jars. Re-cover the jars to prevent further evaporation.

> *If your jam or jelly is too runny, use it as a sauce rather than wasting it.*

- **Runny** jam or jelly is caused by using overripe fruit, insufficient pectin, too much sugar, or not boiling for long enough. Use it as a sauce instead.

APPLE AND BLACKBERRY JAM

This combination of fruits is an old country favorite. Blackberries are low in pectin, but because the apples have a high pectin level, this jam sets well. In late summer and early autumn, blackberries grow profusely in the wild and these have more flavor than the cultivated variety.

TOTAL TIME: 1 HOUR | MAKES: ABOUT SEVEN 8-OZ (250 ML) JARS

- 1 lb 8 oz (680 g) peeled and cored cooking apples
- ⅔ cup (150 mL) water
- 36 oz (1 kg) blackberries
- 3 lbs 2 oz (1.4 kg) granulated or superfine sugar

1. Chop the apples into small pieces, and put them into a large, heavy-based pan with the water. Bring to a boil, then simmer gently for 10 minutes.
2. Add the blackberries. Continue to simmer gently for another 10 minutes until the mixture is a soft purée.
3. Stir in the sugar until completely dissolved, then bring back to a boil. Boil rapidly for about 15–20 minutes until setting point is reached.
4. Remove the pan from the heat. Pour into warmed, sterilized jars, then cover, seal, and label.

APPLE, PEAR, AND PLUM JAM

This was a popular 19th century recipe, and it is a delicious way to use up a glut of seasonal fruit and windfall apples and pears. You can use any variety of fruit in this recipe. Plums come in dozens of varieties, shapes, sizes, and colors, ranging from green to red and deep purple to almost black.

TOTAL TIME: 1 HOUR | MAKES: THREE TO FOUR 32-OZ (1 L) JARS

- 2 lbs (910 g) cooking apples
- 2 lbs (910 g) pears
- 2 lbs (910 g) plums
- Grated zest and juice of 1 lemon
- 5 lbs 1 oz (2.3 kg) granulated or superfine sugar

1. Peel and core the apples and pears. Cut the plums in half and remove the pits. Put all the fruit into a large, heavy-based pan with the lemon zest and juice.

2. Heat gently to the boiling point, then reduce the heat, cover the pan, and simmer very gently until the fruit is soft. If it starts to stick to the pan, add a little water. The actual cooking time needed will depend on the ripeness of the fruit.

3. Stir in the sugar until completely dissolved, then bring to a boil. Boil rapidly for about 15–20 minutes until setting point is reached.

4. Remove the pan from the heat. Pour into warmed, sterilized jars, then cover, seal, and label.

APRICOT JAM

Beautiful orange apricots are one of the first fruits of summer. The fruit is low in pectin, so lemon juice is added to the recipe. You could also use sugar that contains pectin. Add the kernels to the jam just before setting point is reached, otherwise they will become too soft.

TOTAL TIME: 1 HOUR | MAKES: ABOUT FIVE 16-OZ (500 ML) JARS

- 4 lbs 6 oz (2 kg) fresh apricots
- 1¾ cups (450 mL) water
- Juice of 1 lemon
- 4 lbs 6 oz (2 kg) granulated or superfine sugar

1. Cut the apricots in half and remove the pits. Crack 6–8 pits to remove the kernels. Blanch the kernels by dipping them in boiling water for 1 minute. These will give extra flavor to the jam.
2. Put the fruit into a large, heavy-based pan with the water, and bring to a boil. Reduce the heat and simmer gently for about 20 minutes until soft.
3. Stir in the lemon juice and sugar until completely dissolved, then bring to a boil. Boil rapidly for about 15–20 minutes until setting point is reached. Add the kernels to the pan just before setting point is reached.
4. Remove the pan from the heat. Pour into warmed, sterilized jars, then cover, seal, and label.

BANANA JAM

This is a good way of using up a bunch of bananas that is beginning to look a little too brown for the fruit bowl.

TOTAL TIME: 40 MINUTES | MAKES: ABOUT ONE 16-OZ (500 ML) JAR

- 4 ripe bananas
- 2 oz (50 g) chopped cooking apple
- 3 Tbsp (44 mL) water
- 14 oz (400 g) granulated or superfine sugar
- Seeds and juice of 1 large lemon

1. Peel, halve, and slice the bananas lengthways.
2. Put the apple in a large, heavy-based pan with the water and cook until soft.
3. Add the sugar. Then add the lemon juice and seeds, tied in muslin.
4. Cook gently until the sugar has dissolved, bring to a boil, add the bananas, and boil for 10–15 minutes until setting point is reached.
5. Remove the muslin bag. Pour into hot sterilized jars, seal, and label.

BILBERRY (WILD BLUEBERRY) JAM

These small, dark purple berries have a faint dusty "bloom" and are also known as wild blueberries or whortleberries. The berries grow on bushes and have a distinctive, richly aromatic, tart flavor. The skins soften quickly, and their pectin content ensures the jam sets quickly.

TOTAL TIME: 30 MINUTES| MAKES: ABOUT ONE 16-OZ (500 ML) JAR

- 16 oz (450 g) bilberries
- 1 lb (450 g) granulated or superfine sugar

1. Put the bilberries into a large, heavy-based pan. Heat gently to boiling point, then reduce the heat, cover the pan, and simmer very gently for about 10 minutes until the fruit is soft and the juices begin to flow. The actual time will depend on the ripeness of the fruit.

2. Stir in the sugar until completely dissolved, then bring to a boil. Boil rapidly for about 10–15 minutes until setting point is reached.

3. Remove the pan from the heat. Pour into warmed, sterilized jars, then cover, seal, and label.

BLACKCURRANT JAM

These astringent little blue-black berries grow on shrubs and have a sweet-sharp flavor. They have high levels of health-boosting antioxidants—natural compounds (responsible for the fruit's dark color) that are credited with the ability to stave off a range of illnesses.

TOTAL TIME: 1 HOUR 10 MINUTES | MAKES: ABOUT THREE 8-OZ (250 ML) JARS

- 16 oz (450 g) blackcurrants
- 1¼–1¾ cups (300–450 mL) water
- 1 lb 3 oz (550 g) granulated or superfine sugar

1. Strip the berries from their stalks with a fork into a large, heavy-based pan. Add the water and slowly bring to a boil. Reduce the heat and simmer gently for about 20–30 minutes until the fruit is soft.

2. Add the sugar, and stir over a low heat until the sugar has dissolved completely. Bring to a boil, and boil rapidly for about 10–15 minutes until setting point is reached.

3. Remove the pan from the heat. Pour into warmed, sterilized jars, then cover, seal, and label.

CHERRY JAM

Cherries can be bright red, pale pink, yellow, or very dark, almost black. Small, dark red wild cherries are also known as "geans" (from the French *guine*) and may be sweet or bitter. Leaving the cherry pits in while you cook them imparts a delicate almond flavor to the finished jam.

TOTAL TIME: 1 HOUR 10 MINUTES | MAKES: ABOUT ONE 16-OZ (500 ML) JAR

- 1 lb 8 oz (680 g) firm dessert cherries
- 2 Tbsp (30 mL) water
- 1 Tbsp (15 mL) lemon juice
- 14 oz (400 g) granulated or superfine sugar

1. Put the cherries into a large, heavy-based pan with the water. The pits add flavor to the jam and can be removed when the jam is boiling.
2. Heat gently to boiling point, then reduce the heat, cover the pan, and simmer very gently until the fruit is soft. If it starts to stick to the pan, add a little more water. The actual time will depend on the ripeness of the fruit.
3. Stir in the lemon juice and sugar until completely dissolved, then bring to a boil. Boil rapidly for about 15–20 minutes until setting point is reached.
4. Remove the pan from the heat, then remove the pits with a slotted spoon. Allow to stand for a few minutes, and stir to distribute the fruit. Pour into warmed, sterilized jars, then cover, seal, and label.

GOOSEBERRY AND ELDERFLOWER JAM

Although red and yellow varieties of gooseberry are sweeter than green, the small, hard, green berries are best for cooking because they have more flavor. The raw berries are sharp and sour tasting, but their acidity is transformed when cooking them with sugar. Elderflowers add a delicate muscat flavor. Pick the creamy white flowers well away from the roadside and traffic fumes, give them a gentle shake to dislodge any insects, and rinse briefly in cold water before using.

TOTAL TIME: 1 HOUR 10 MINUTES | MAKES: ABOUT TWO 32-OZ (1 L) JARS

- 53 oz (1.5 kg) hard, slightly underripe gooseberries, topped and tailed
- 2 small heads of elderflowers, stems removed and tied in muslin
- 2½ cups (600 mL) water
- 3 lbs 5 oz (1.5 kg) granulated or superfine sugar

1. Put the gooseberries, elderflowers, and water into a large, heavy-based pan.
2. Heat gently to boiling point, then reduce the heat. Cover the pan, and simmer very gently for about 20–30 minutes until the skins are soft, stirring from time to time to prevent the fruit from sticking. The actual time will depend on the ripeness of the fruit.
3. Stir in the sugar until completely dissolved, then bring to a boil. Boil rapidly for about 15–20 minutes until setting point is reached.
4. Remove the pan from the heat, then discard the elderflowers. Pour into warmed, sterilized jars, then cover, seal, and label.

GREENGAGE JAM

Greengages are small- to medium-sized plums with a tender green-yellow or golden skin. The translucent golden flesh is wonderfully sweet. The fruit is high in pectin and produces superb jam.

TOTAL TIME: 1 HOUR 10 MINUTES| MAKES: ABOUT FOUR 32-OZ (1 L) JARS

- 6 lbs 10 oz (3 kg) greengages
- 2½ cups (600 mL) water
- 6 lbs 10 oz (3 kg) granulated or superfine sugar

1. Cut the fruit in half and remove the pits. If the fruit is too firm to remove the pits easily, cook the fruit with the pits in and remove them with a slotted spoon when the jam is boiling.
2. Crack 8–10 pits to remove the kernels. Blanch the kernels by dipping them in boiling water for 1 minute. These will give extra flavor to the jam.
3. Put the fruit into a large, heavy-based pan with the water, and bring to a boil. Reduce the heat, and simmer gently for about 30 minutes until soft. The actual time will depend on the ripeness of the fruit.
4. Stir in the sugar until completely dissolved, then bring to a boil. Boil rapidly for about 15–20 minutes until setting point is reached. Add the kernels to the pan just before setting point is reached.
5. Remove the pan from the heat. Pour into warmed, sterilized jars, then cover, seal, and label.

MICROWAVE STRAWBERRY JAM

The microwave is wonderful for making jam. This recipe uses the last of the summer strawberries that are overripe or a little past their best, which are ideal for jam. Don't try to make larger quantities than the amount here, and test often during cooking. Cooking times are based on an 800-watt microwave. The length of cooking time varies and depends on the size of bowl used and ripeness of the fruit.

TOTAL TIME: 30 MINUTES, PLUS 5 MINUTES STANDING | MAKES: ABOUT THREE 4-OZ (125 ML) JARS

- 16 oz (450 g) strawberries
- ¼ cup (55 mL) lemon juice
- 1 lb (450 g) granulated or superfine sugar

1. Wash and hull the strawberries. Place in a very large microwaveable bowl with the lemon juice.
2. Cook on high for 4 minutes or until the fruit is soft.
3. Stir in the sugar. When completely dissolved, cook until the jam sets when tested on a chilled saucer, stirring every 3 minutes. This will take about 15–20 minutes.
4. Stand for 5 minutes, and then pour into hot sterilized jars, seal, and label.

MIDDLE EASTERN FIG JAM

A fragrant jam that's delicious when spread on bread or eaten with goat cheese.

TOTAL TIME: 25 MINUTES, PLUS 30 MINUTES STANDING | MAKES: ABOUT ONE 16-OZ (500 ML) JAR

- 1 lb 2 oz (500 g) fresh figs, chopped
- 4 oz (110 g) granulated sugar
- Squeeze of lemon juice
- ½ tsp ground cinnamon
- ½ tsp ground cardamom
- ½ tsp (2.5 mL) rose water
- ½ tsp (2.5 mL) orange flower water
- Splash of white wine
- 2 Tbsp (30 mL) water

1. Put the figs, sugar, lemon juice, spices, and flower waters in a bowl. Leave to stand for at least 30 minutes.
2. Put the mixture into a pan, add the wine and water, and bring to a boil over a medium heat, stirring constantly. Reduce the heat and simmer for about 15 mins until the jam is thick.
3. Pour into hot sterilized jars, cover, seal, and label.

MULBERRY AND PLUM JAM

Dark crimson mulberries make a luxurious and unusual jam. The medium to large fruit has a yellow-to-rose-colored skin. The pinkish flesh is rich, sweet, and juicy when ripe. Before the fruit is fully ripe, it is particularly good for making excellent jam. Blackberries are a good substitute.

TOTAL TIME: 1 HOUR | MAKES: ABOUT THREE 16-OZ (500 ML) JARS

- 36 oz (1 kg) mulberries
- 2 lbs 3 oz (1 kg) Victoria plums
- 1¼ cups (300 mL) water
- Granulated or superfine sugar (see step 2)
- Juice of 1 lemon
- 2 Tbsp (28 g) unsalted butter

1. Put the mulberries and plums in a large, heavy-based pan with the water, and bring to a boil. Reduce the heat and simmer gently until soft.
2. Press the mixture through a sieve into a bowl. In a measuring cup, measure the mixture back into the pan. For every 2½ cups (600 mL) of fruit mixture, add 1 lb (450 g) of sugar.
3. Add the lemon juice and bring slowly to a boil, then boil rapidly for about 15–20 minutes until setting point is reached.
4. Remove the pan from the heat and stir in the butter. Allow to stand for 5 minutes. Pour into warmed, sterilized jars, then cover, seal, and label.

PEACH AND WALNUT JAM

Velvet-skinned, fresh, juicy peaches and crisp-textured walnuts are combined to make an unusual jam with a delightful flavor. Old gardens yield rich-tasting walnuts with crinkled surfaces. When young, they have a fresh, milky flavor and better texture than some available in stores.

TOTAL TIME: 1 HOUR | MAKES: ABOUT FIVE 8-OZ (250 ML) JARS

- 1 lb (450 g) ripe peaches
- 1 lb (450 g) ripe fruit, such as pears, apples, etc.
- 1 lb 8 oz (680 g) granulated or superfine sugar
- 2 oz (50 g) walnuts, chopped

1. Peel all the fruit and cut into small pieces. Put into a large, heavy-based pan with the sugar. Stir over a low heat until completely dissolved, then bring to a boil. Boil rapidly for about 15–20 minutes until thick and setting point is reached.

2. Stir in the walnuts and boil for 1 minute.

3. Remove the pan from the heat. Pour into warmed, sterilized jars, then cover, seal, and label.

RASPBERRY JAM

Red or yellow raspberries are among summer's most delicious fruits. Make the most of their fleeting appearance with this beautiful scarlet jam. When sugar became affordable to all in the 18th century, it became very fashionable to make jams and preserves from these berries.

TOTAL TIME: 40 MINUTES | MAKES: ABOUT FIVE 16-OZ (500 ML) JARS

- 70 oz (2 kg) raspberries
- 4 lbs 6 oz (2 kg) granulated or superfine sugar

1. Put the raspberries into a large, heavy-based pan. Crush the fruit with a wooden spoon to release the juices. Heat gently to boiling point, then simmer until the juices run.
2. Stir in the sugar until completely dissolved, then bring to a boil.
3. If you prefer a seedless jam, press the fruit and juices through a sieve and return to the rinsed pan. Boil rapidly for about 8–12 minutes until setting point is reached.
4. Remove the pan from the heat. Pour into warmed, sterilized jars, then cover, seal, and label.

RHUBARB AND GINGER JAM

The sharp, fresh taste of rhubarb has a special affinity with ginger. Limp rhubarb can be perked up by standing the stems upright in iced water for about an hour.

NOTE: Rhubarb leaves contain oxalic acid, so are highly poisonous and must be discarded.

TOTAL TIME: 35 MINUTES, PLUS 24 HOURS STANDING | MAKES: ABOUT THREE 24-OZ (750 ML) JARS

- 3 lbs 5 oz (1.5 kg) rhubarb, chopped into small pieces
- Juice of 1 lemon
- 2 lbs 14 oz (1.3 kg) granulated or superfine sugar
- 3 Tbsp (120 g) crystallized ginger, chopped

1. Put the rhubarb, lemon juice, and sugar into a large bowl. Cover and leave to stand for 24 hours.
2. Tip the mixture into a large pan and add the ginger. Heat very gently over a low heat until the sugar has dissolved completely, then increase the heat and bring to a boil. Boil rapidly for about 20 minutes until setting point is reached.
3. Remove the pan from the heat. Pour into warmed, sterilized jars, then cover, seal, and label.

ROSE PETAL JAM

A sweet jam with a delicate-scented flavor. Use heavily perfumed rose petals, but make sure they have not been sprayed with insecticide.

TOTAL TIME: 25 MINUTES | MAKES: ABOUT ONE 16-OZ (500 ML) JAR

- 8 oz (227 g) rose petals
- 8 oz (227 g) granulated sugar
- 4 Tbsp (60 mL) water
- ½ Tbsp (8 mL) lemon juice
- ½ Tbsp (8 mL) rose water

1. Remove the white "heel" at the base of the petals, as this is bitter tasting. Cut the petals into small pieces, and put into a large, heavy-based pan with the sugar, water, and lemon juice.
2. Place over a very low heat until the sugar has dissolved.
3. Bring to a boil and cook until setting point is reached. Cool slightly, then stir in the rose water.
4. Pour into warm sterilized jars and cover and seal immediately.

STRAWBERRY JAM

Strawberries are plentiful in the summer and their sunny-scented, fruity flavor makes for superb jam. Rinse the fruits very gently, and hull the berries after washing to avoid making them soggy.

TOTAL TIME: 1 HOUR | MAKES: FOUR TO FIVE 16-OZ (500 ML) JARS

- 70 oz (2 kg) strawberries
- 3 lbs 8 oz (1.6 kg) granulated or superfine sugar
- Juice of 2 large lemons (about ½ cup [118 mL])

1. Cut any very large strawberries into smaller pieces to speed up the cooking time. Put the strawberries into a large, heavy-based pan over a low heat, and slowly bring to a boil. Reduce the heat and simmer gently for about 10–15 minutes until the fruit is softened.

2. Add the sugar and lemon juice. Stir over a low heat until the sugar has dissolved completely. Bring to a boil, and boil rapidly for about 15–20 minutes until setting point is reached.

3. Remove the pan from the heat. Skim off any foam, and allow the jam to cool for 15 minutes to ensure the strawberries are distributed evenly. Pour into warmed, sterilized jars, then cover, seal, and label.

TOMATO APPLE JAM

Botanically, the tomato is really a fruit and many people used to eat them as a fruit in the past. Tomato jams were popular at the end of the 19th century, when the tomatoes were often combined with other fruit. This sweet preserve is delicious as an accompaniment to cakes or scones.

TOTAL TIME: 45 MINUTES | MAKES: ABOUT FIVE 8-OZ (250 ML) JARS

- 1 lb (450 g) cooking apples (peeled and cored weight)
- 1 lb (450 g) red tomatoes, skinned and finely chopped
- 3 Tbsp (44 mL) water
- 2 lbs 3 oz (1 kg) granulated or superfine sugar

1. Chop the apples finely and put into a large, heavy-based pan with the tomatoes and water. Bring to a boil, then simmer gently for about 15 minutes until the fruits are soft and mushy.

2. Stir in the sugar until completely dissolved, then bring to a boil. Boil rapidly for about 15–20 minutes until setting point is reached.

3. Remove the pan from the heat. Pour into warmed, sterilized jars, then cover, seal, and label.

Uncooked Raspberry Jam

All the wonderful flavor of fresh raspberries is preserved in this easy to make jam which is stored in the freezer. You can also use strawberries in this way.

TOTAL TIME: 20 MINUTES, PLUS 7 HOURS STANDING AND 1–2 DAYS CHILLING
MAKES: ABOUT NINE 4-OZ (125 ML) JARS

- 36 oz (1 kg) raspberries
- 1 lb (450 g) jam sugar
- Juice of 1 lemon

1. Place the raspberries in a nonmetallic bowl and crush them with a wooden spoon.
2. Stir in the sugar, cover the bowl, and put into the oven set at the lowest setting until warm, but do not allow to become hot.
3. Remove from the oven and leave to stand for 1 hour, stirring occasionally until the sugar has dissolved. Stir in the lemon juice.
4. Pack the mixture into small freezer proof containers, leaving plenty of room for expansion. Cover, seal, and leave at room temperature for 6 hours.
5. Place in the refrigerator to chill for 1–2 days until jellied. Store in the freezer. Thaw for 1 hour before serving. Once thawed, the jam will keep in the refrigerator for 2–3 days.

ZUCCHINI AND GINGER JAM

As the zucchini grows, it swells up with water, so the flesh is watery with a very delicate, almost insipid flavor. Zucchinis have long been used to make jam, and ginger is usually included to add a kick.

TOTAL TIME: 50 MINUTES, PLUS STANDING OVERNIGHT | MAKES: ABOUT FIVE 16-OZ (500 ML) JARS

- 4 lbs 6 oz (2 kg) peeled and seeded zucchini
- 4 lbs 6 oz (2 kg) granulated or superfine sugar
- 6 Tbsp (240 g) crystallized ginger, finely chopped
- Juice of 3 lemons

1. Cut the zucchini into small pieces. Put into a large, heavy-based pan with the sugar and ginger. Cover and leave overnight.

2. Stir well and place over a low heat, stirring until the sugar has dissolved completely. Add the lemon juice and bring to a boil. Boil steadily for about 30 minutes until setting point is reached.

3. Remove the pan from the heat. Allow to stand for a few minutes, and stir to distribute the zucchini pieces. Pour into warmed, sterilized jars, then cover, seal, and label.

BRAMBLE (BLACKBERRY) JELLY

Brambles or blackberries are low in pectin, so lemon juice is essential in this recipe. To help the jelly set, you can include some unripe red blackberries if you wish. This dark purple jelly is wonderful as a filling for sponge cakes or as an accompaniment to roast lamb.

TOTAL TIME: 1 HOUR 20 MINUTES, PLUS STRAINING OVERNIGHT | MAKES: ABOUT THREE 8-OZ (250 ML) JARS

- 36 oz (1 kg) blackberries
- ⅔ cup (150 mL) water
- Granulated or superfine sugar (see step 3)
- Lemon juice (see step 3)

1. Put the blackberries (there's no need to top and tail them) into a large, heavy-based pan with the water. Place over a low heat and slowly bring to a boil. Reduce the heat and simmer gently for about 40–60 minutes until the fruit is very soft.
2. Ladle the fruit and juices into a scalded jelly bag. Strain through the jelly bag overnight.
3. Measure the juice into a large, heavy-based pan. For every 2½ cups (600 mL) juice, add 1 lb (450 g) sugar and 2 Tbsp (30 mL) lemon juice.
4. Heat the juice, sugar, and lemon juice, and stir over a low heat until the sugar has dissolved completely. Bring to a boil and boil rapidly for about 10 minutes until setting point is reached.
5. Remove the pan from the heat. Pour into warmed, sterilized jars, then cover, seal, and label.

CRABAPPLE JELLY

Small, hard crabapples are high in pectin and make one of the best wild fruit jellies. The color of the jelly can range from pink to yellow-green, depending on the variety of crabapple. It is delicious served with cold ham, poultry, or scones and whipped cream.

TOTAL TIME: 1 HOUR 45 MINUTES, PLUS STRAINING OVERNIGHT | MAKES: ABOUT FIVE 8-OZ (250 ML) JARS

- 4 lbs 6 oz (2 kg) crabapples, cut into quarters
- 5 cups (1.2 L) water
- Granulated or superfine sugar (see step 3)

1. Put the crabapples (there's no need to peel or core them) into a large, heavy-based pan with the water. Place over a low heat and slowly bring to a boil. Reduce the heat, and simmer gently for about 1½ hours until the fruit is soft and pulpy.

2. Ladle the fruit and juices into a scalded jelly bag. Strain through the jelly bag overnight.

3. Measure the juice into a large, heavy-based pan. For every 2½ cups (600 mL) juice, add 1 lb (450 g) sugar.

4. Heat the juice and sugar, and stir over a low heat until the sugar has dissolved completely. Bring to a boil and boil rapidly for about 10–20 minutes until setting point is reached.

5. Remove the pan from the heat. Pour into warmed, sterilized jars, then cover, seal, and label.

GOOSEBERRY MINT JELLY

Gooseberry jelly has been served with oily fish, such as mackerel, and fatty meats, such as pork, lamb, and duck. Use a mild mint.

TOTAL TIME: 45 MINUTES, PLUS STRAINING OVERNIGHT | MAKES: ABOUT THREE 8-OZ (250 ML) JARS

- 36 oz (1 kg) hard, green gooseberries
- Water, as needed
- Granulated or superfine sugar (see step 3)
- 6–8 sprigs mint, tied into a bundle
- Juice of 2 lemons

1. Put the gooseberries into a large, heavy-based pan (there's no need to top and tail them) and just cover with water. Place over a low heat and slowly bring to a boil. Reduce the heat and simmer gently for about 15–20 minutes until the fruit is soft.
2. Ladle the fruit and juices into a scalded jelly bag. Strain through the jelly bag overnight.
3. Measure the juice into a large, heavy-based pan. For every 2½ cups (600 mL) juice, add 1 lb (450 g) sugar.
4. Heat the juice, sugar, mint, and lemon juice, and stir over a low heat until the sugar has dissolved completely. Bring to a boil and boil rapidly for about 10–20 minutes until setting point is reached. Remove the mint.
5. Remove the pan from the heat. Pour into warmed, sterilized jars, then cover, seal, and label.

HERB JELLY

You can use a single herb or a mixture of herbs for this savory jelly. Sage is delicious with pork; parsley with ham; thyme with poultry; and rosemary or mint with lamb. Mixed herb jelly is delicious served with fish or with soft cheeses, such as goat cheese.

TOTAL TIME: 2 HOURS, PLUS STRAINING OVERNIGHT | MAKES: ABOUT THREE 8-OZ (250 ML) JARS

- 3 lbs 5 oz (1.5 kg) cooking apples, coarsely chopped
- 3¾ cups (900 mL) water
- 6–8 sprigs fresh herbs, tied into a bundle
- ⅔ cup (150 mL) white malt or white wine vinegar
- Granulated or superfine sugar (see step 4)
- 4 Tbsp (25 g) chopped fresh herbs

1. Put the apples into a large, heavy-based pan with the water and herb bundle. Place over a low heat and slowly bring to a boil. Reduce the heat and simmer gently for about 1 hour until the fruit is soft, stirring occasionally.

2. Add the vinegar and cook for another 5 minutes. Mash the fruit to a pulp.

3. Ladle the fruit and juices into a scalded jelly bag. Strain through the jelly bag overnight.

4. Measure the juice into a large, heavy-based pan. For every 2½ cups (600 mL) juice, add 1 lb (450 g) sugar.

5. Heat the juice and sugar. Stir over a low heat until the sugar has dissolved completely. Bring to a boil and boil rapidly for about 10 minutes until setting point is reached.

6. Remove the pan from the heat. Add the chopped herbs, and leave to stand for 5–10 minutes until a skin has formed on the surface. Stir once, pour into warmed, sterilized jars, then cover, seal, and label.

MEDLAR JELLY

A member of the rose family, medlars are brown pear-shaped fruits with hard, rough skins and a lightly spicy, tart flavor. After picking, the fruit must be allowed to blett—that is, become soft and brown inside before they can be eaten raw. The jelly can be made with ripe or slightly unripe fruit and is excellent with game, or with scones and whipped cream.

TOTAL TIME: 1 HOUR 20 MINUTES, PLUS STRAINING OVERNIGHT | MAKES: ABOUT FIVE 8-OZ (250 ML) JARS

- 4 lbs 6 oz (2 kg) medlars, chopped
- 7⅓ cups (1.8 L) water
- 1 large lemon
- Granulated or superfine sugar (see step 3)
- Lemon juice, if needed

1. Put the medlars (there's no need to peel them or remove the seeds) into a large, heavy-based pan and just cover with water. Place over a low heat and slowly bring to a boil. Reduce the heat and simmer gently for about 20–30 minutes until the fruit is reduced to a brown pulp.

2. Ladle the fruit and juices into a scalded jelly bag. Strain through the jelly bag overnight.

3. Measure the juice into a large, heavy-based pan. For every 2½ cups (600 mL) juice, add 1 lb (450 g) sugar. If using very ripe fruit, add 2 Tbsp (30 mL) to the pan.

4. Heat the juice, sugar, and lemon juice (if using), and stir over a low heat until the sugar has dissolved completely. Bring to a boil and boil rapidly for about 20–25 minutes until setting point is reached.

5. Remove the pan from the heat. Pour into warmed, sterilized jars, then cover, seal, and label.

QUINCE JELLY

Wonderfully perfumed quinces are hard and inedible when raw but delectable when cooked, when the flesh becomes deep pink. As this jelly cooks, it will fill the house with a wonderful aroma. Add a spoonful of quince jelly to apple pies or crumbles before cooking or serve with roast meats and game. If using very ripe fruit, use the smaller amount of water and the maximum if the fruit is hard.

TOTAL TIME: 1 HOUR 20 MINUTES, PLUS STRAINING OVERNIGHT | MAKES: ABOUT THREE 8-OZ (250 ML) JARS

- 2 lbs 3 oz (1 kg) quinces
- 3¾–6¼ cups (900 mL–1.5 L) water
- Granulated or superfine sugar (see step 3)

1. Wash the quinces and scrub away the grayish down (there's no need to peel or core them). Cut them roughly into pieces and put them into a large, heavy-based pan with the water. Place over a low heat and slowly bring to a boil. Reduce the heat and simmer gently for about 40–50 minutes until the fruit is reduced to a pulp.

2. Ladle the fruit and juices into a scalded jelly bag. Strain through the jelly bag overnight.

3. Measure the juice into a large, heavy-based pan. For every 2½ cups (600 mL) juice, add 1 lb (450 g) sugar.

4. Heat the juice and sugar, and stir over a low heat until the sugar has dissolved completely. Bring to a boil and boil rapidly for about 15 minutes until setting point is reached.

5. Remove the pan from the heat. Pour into warmed, sterilized jars, then cover, seal, and label.

REDCURRANT AND ROSEMARY JELLY

Scarlet, translucent redcurrant jelly is delicious with game and roast lamb. Rosemary is added to the traditional recipe to give a lovely aromatic flavor to the sweet jelly. Add a spoonful of this jelly to the gravy of lamb or game for extra flavor.

TOTAL TIME: 1 HOUR PLUS STRAINING OVERNIGHT | MAKES: ABOUT THREE 8-OZ (250 ML) JARS

- 53 oz (1.5 kg) redcurrants
- 2½ cups (600 mL) water
- Granulated or superfine sugar (see step 3)
- 3–4 Tbsp (19–25 g) rosemary leaves, chopped

1. Put the redcurrants (there's no need to remove the stalks) into a large, heavy-based pan with the water. Place over a low heat and slowly bring to a boil. Reduce the heat and simmer gently for about 20–30 minutes until the fruit is very soft.

2. Ladle the fruit and juices into a scalded jelly bag. Strain through the jelly bag overnight.

3. Measure the juice into a large, heavy-based pan. For every 2½ cups (600 mL) juice, add 1 lb (450 g) sugar. Heat the juice and sugar, and stir over a low heat until the sugar has dissolved completely.

4. Add the rosemary, bring to a boil and boil rapidly for about 10–20 minutes until setting point is reached.

5. Remove the pan from the heat. Pour into warmed, sterilized jars, then cover, seal, and label.

ROWAN JELLY

Rowanberries are the fruit of the mountain ash tree. The orange red berries make a tangy jelly with a hint of bitterness, which is traditionally served as an accompaniment to game, particularly venison. It is also delicious with other meats.

TOTAL TIME: 1 HOUR 15 MINUTES PLUS STRAINING OVERNIGHT | MAKES: ABOUT THREE 8-OZ (250 ML) JARS

- 36 oz (1 kg) rowanberries
- 1¼ cups (300 mL) water
- Granulated or superfine sugar (see step 3)

1. Put the rowanberries (there's no need to peel and core them) into a large, heavy-based pan with the water. Place over a low heat and slowly bring to a boil. Reduce the heat and simmer gently for about 30–40 minutes until the fruit is very soft.

2. Ladle the fruit and juices into a scalded jelly bag. Strain through the jelly bag overnight.

3. Measure the juice into a large, heavy-based pan. For every 2½ cups (600 mL) juice, allow 1 lb (450 g) sugar.

4. Heat the juice and sugar, and stir over a low heat until the sugar has dissolved completely. Bring to a boil and boil rapidly for about 10–15 minutes until setting point is reached.

5. Remove the pan from the heat. Pour into warmed, sterilized jars, then cover, seal, and label.

JAMS, JELLIES, AND MARMALADES **49**

GRAPEFRUIT AND LEMON MARMALADE

Made from two tartly refreshing citrus fruits, this marmalade has a wonderful fruity flavor. The citrus zing and sharp fragrance of tangy grapefruit and lemons make a peppy preserve. Citrus fruits may be waxed to protect them from bruising during shipping; because the peel is used, it is best to use organically grow lemons and limes, which are unwaxed. Wash the fruit, scrubbing the skin to remove any dirt or bacteria on the surface, and dry well.

TOTAL TIME: 3 HOURS | MAKES: ABOUT TWO 32-OZ (1 L) JARS

- 2 lbs 3 oz (1 kg) grapefruit, scrubbed
- 1 lb (450 g) lemons, scrubbed
- 7 cups (1.7 L) water
- 3 lbs 5 oz (1.5 kg) granulated or superfine sugar, warmed in a very low oven

1. Place the fruit in boiling water for 3 minutes (this makes the fruit easier to peel). Remove from the water and peel with a potato peeler. Cut the peel into fine shreds and put into a large, heavy-based pan.

2. Remove the pith from the fruit and chop the flesh roughly. Add the flesh to the pan together with any juice from the fruit.

3. Place the pith and seeds in a muslin bag and add to the pan with the water. Place over a low heat and slowly bring to a boil. Reduce the heat and simmer gently for 1½–2 hours until the peel is tender. Remove the pan from the heat, and squeeze the muslin bag into the mixture before discarding it.

4. Stir in the warmed sugar until completely dissolved and then bring to a boil. Boil rapidly for about 10–15 minutes until setting point is reached.

5. Remove the pan from the heat. Skim off any scum from the surface and leave to stand for 10–20 minutes. Stir once, pour into warmed, sterilized jars, then cover, seal, and label.

LIME MARMALADE

Limes make a very tasty marmalade. They have less juice than lemons, so lemon juice is added to the recipe. Choose limes that are firm and heavy for their size, with deep-green, shiny skin when their sharp, tart flavor is at its best.

TOTAL TIME: 2 HOURS 10 MINUTES | MAKES: ABOUT THREE 16-OZ (500 ML) JARS

- 1 lb 11 oz (675 g) limes, scrubbed
- 7 cups (1.7 L) water
- 1½ Tbsp (22 mL) lemon juice
- 3 lbs 5 oz (1.5 kg) granulated or superfine sugar, warmed in a very low oven

1. Place the limes in boiling water for 3 minutes (this makes the fruit easier to peel). Remove the rind from the limes with a potato peeler and cut into fine shreds.
2. Remove the pith and chop the flesh. Place the pith and seeds in a muslin bag and add to the pan with the water. Place over a low heat and slowly bring to a boil. Reduce the heat and simmer gently for 1–1½ hours until the peel is tender. Remove the pan from the heat, and squeeze the muslin bag into the mixture before discarding it.
3. Stir in the lemon juice and warm sugar, and cook over a low heat, stirring all the time until completely dissolved. Bring to a boil and boil rapidly for about 10–15 minutes until setting point is reached.
4. Remove the pan from the heat. Skim off any foam from the surface and leave to stand for 10 minutes. Stir once, pour into warmed, sterilized jars, then cover, seal, and label.

MICROWAVE CITRUS MARMALADE

A tangy marmalade packed with fresh citrus flavor.

TOTAL TIME: 1 HOUR, PLUS 2 HOURS STANDING | MAKES: ABOUT ONE 16-OZ (500 ML) JAR

- 2 Seville oranges
- 1 lemon
- 1 lime
- 2 cups (500 mL) boiling water
- 1 lb 10 oz (750 g) sugar, warmed

1. Cut the fruits in half and slice thinly. Put into a large microwaveable bowl.
2. Remove the excess pith and seeds from the fruits, put into a muslin bag, and add to the bowl with the water.
3. Cover with clingfilm and leave to stand for at least 2 hours or overnight.
4. Cook, covered, in the microwave on full power for 15 minutes, stirring halfway through.
5. Strain the muslin bag into the fruit, pressing well to extract the maximum pectin.
6. Stir in the sugar until completely dissolved. Cook uncovered on full power for 20 minutes, without stirring until setting point is reached.
7. Pour into hot sterilized jars, seal, and label. Store for up to 1 month in the refrigerator.

SEVILLE ORANGE MARMALADE

Bitter or Seville oranges are highly scented with gloriously fragrant aromatic peel and astringent juice. The fruit inspired the creation of Curaçao liqueur and orange marmalade. Using a sweet orange would be too insipid, and it would lack the depth of flavor needed for this superb marmalade.

TOTAL TIME: 3 HOURS | MAKES: ABOUT SEVEN 16-OZ (500 ML) JARS

- 3 lbs 5 oz (1.5 kg) Seville oranges, scrubbed
- Juice of 2 lemons
- 14 cups (3.4 L) water
- 6 lbs 10 oz (3 kg) granulated or superfine sugar, warmed in a very low oven

1. Cut the oranges in half and squeeze out the juice and seeds. Scoop out the flesh and reserve. Cut away any thick white pith from the peel, and finely shred the peel with a sharp knife.

2. Put the shredded peel, orange, lemon juices, muslin bag, and water into a large, heavy-based pan. Place over a low heat and slowly bring to a boil. Reduce the heat and simmer gently for 1½–2 hours until the peel is tender.

3. Stir in the warmed sugar until completely dissolved and then bring to a boil. Boil rapidly for about 15 minutes until setting point is reached.

4. Remove the pan from the heat. Skim off any scum from the surface, and leave to stand for 10–20 minutes. Stir once, pour into warmed, sterilized jars, then cover, seal, and label.

PARSLEY HONEY

Parsley has a fresh, green, vibrant flavor. This is an old country recipe used when honey was in short supply or was difficult to obtain. Parsley honey was a popular substitute for the real thing and can be used wherever you would use honey. It's delicious spread on scones or toast.

TOTAL TIME: 1 HOUR 10 MINUTES | MAKES: ABOUT ONE 16-OZ (500 ML) JAR

- 5 oz (150 g) fresh parsley
- 3½ cups (850 mL) water
- 1 lb (450 g) granulated or superfine sugar
- ½ tsp (2.5 mL) white malt or white wine vinegar, or juice of 1 small lemon

1. Wash the parsley well and dry thoroughly. Chop it roughly, including the stalks, and put into a large, heavy-based pan with the water. Place over a low heat and slowly bring to a boil. Boil steadily for about 30 minutes until the liquid is reduced to 2½ cups (600 mL).
2. Strain the mixture into a clean pan and add the sugar. Heat gently until the sugar has dissolved completely, then bring to a boil. Cook steadily for about 20 minutes until clear and syrupy, like thin honey. Stir in the vinegar or lemon juice.
3. Remove from the heat. Pour into warmed, sterilized jars, then cover, seal, and label. The mixture will set overnight.

Fruit Butters
and Curds

Fruit butters and curds are traditional preserves
that were originally made to use up extra fruit and
intended to be eaten fairly quickly, as they don't
keep as well as jams. Delicious spread on bread and
butter, they also make excellent fillings for tarts
and cakes.

Tasty dessert rolls with lemon curd.

Equipment

- **A durable bowl**. The options I recommend are a heavy-based or double saucepan, or a heatproof bowl.
- A **fine sieve** to remove any lumps.
- **Sterilized glass jars** (page 13) with metal or plastic covers or lids. Fruit butters are not covered with waxed discs but with airtight metal or plastic lids only.

A fine sieve helps remove any lumps during the process.

Ingredients

Almost any fruit is suitable. Homemade lemon curd made from fresh lemons has a much better flavor than commercial brands. Lemons have a refreshingly sharp citrus flavor. Choose thin-skinned fruits (those with a thicker peel will have less flesh and therefore be less juicy) that are heavy for their size and bright yellow. Avoid any that are tinged with green, as they're not fully ripe and will be very acidic. Use unwaxed citrus fruits if possible; otherwise, the fruit must be well scrubbed under hot running water to remove the protective waxy coating of fungicide. Use a potato peeler to remove the rind in thin strips, and don't include the white pith as this is very bitter.

Limes are oval or round with green flesh and skin, and they are more fragrant than lemons. Choose limes that are firm and heavy for their size with deep green, shiny skin. Use unwaxed fruits if possible.

The flavor of homemade lemon curd is much better than store bought.

Fresh eggs that are about two days old are best for butters and curds.

Some fruit butters and curds are made with low amounts of sugar and so will not keep for very long. Use fresh eggs, but not newly laid: about two days old is ideal. This is because very fresh eggs have a high moisture content, which will prevent the mixture from thickening. Eggs with deep-colored yolks are best for lemon curd. Use unsalted butter, otherwise the curd will be slightly salty.

Some fruit butters and curds are made with low amounts of sugar and so won't keep for long.

Curd is thick when mixed, but it will thicken more once cooled.

Cooking

The ingredients are cooked together until the mixture becomes stiff, thick, and smooth. Mixtures containing egg yolks are cooked in a double saucepan or heatproof bowl over a pan of simmering (but not boiling) water; this prevents the egg from overcooking and the mixture from curdling and separating. The water must not touch the base of the bowl, as too much heat will be transferred and it will cause the mixture to boil, spoiling the curd. When cool, the curd becomes thick enough to spread.

Check that the sugar has dissolved completely. The mixture should be thick enough to coat the back of a spoon.

As a general guide, fruit curd is ready when a spoon drawn across the surface of the mixture leaves a clean line. Fruit butter is ready when no free liquid is visible and the surface is creamy.

It is difficult to estimate how much preserve a recipe will make, as this depends on how juicy the fruit is. As a general guide, 1 lb (450 g) sugar should make about 1 lb 10 oz (750 g) or one 32-oz (1 L) jar of fruit butter or curd.

Spoon the mixture into sterilized jars right up to the top, as the mixture will shrink a little as it cools.

The jars are then sealed and labeled in the same way as for jam (page 18). The jars must be stored in the refrigerator and eaten within two to three weeks. Once opened, the curds or butters should be eaten with a few days.

WHAT CAN GO WRONG?

Curdling (separating) occurs in preserves made with eggs if the mixture becomes too hot. The mixture should be cooked very slowly, stirring continuously in a double saucepan or bowl over a pan of simmering water so that the mixture doesn't come into contact with direct heat. If the mixture curdles, remove from the heat immediately and whisk vigorously to amalgamate the mixture again. Continue to whisk until thick.

Mold occurs if the preserve is kept in a warm or damp place. Fruit butters and curds should be kept in the refrigerator and eaten within three weeks. Inspect regularly for signs of mold.

APPLE BUTTER

Cooking apples have a sharp, tart flavor and retain their shape well during cooking. Apple butter is lightly spiced and delicious spread on scones, bread, or toast, and also as a filling for sponge cakes. Using cider instead of water produces a more pronounced apple flavor.

TOTAL TIME: 1 HOUR 15 MINUTES | MAKES: ABOUT TWO 16-OZ (500 ML) JARS PER 1 LB (450 G) SUGAR

- 3 lbs 5 oz (1.5 kg) cooking apples, coarsely chopped, including cores and peel
- 4 cups (1.1 L) water or cider
- Pinch of ground cloves
- ½ tsp ground cinnamon
- 12 oz (350 g) granulated or superfine sugar for each 1 lb (450 g) fruit pulp (see step 2)

1. Put the apples (including cores and peel) into a large, heavy-based pan, and cover with the water or cider. Bring to a boil and simmer gently for about 30 minutes until very soft.
2. Remove the pan from the heat. Push the mixture through a sieve into a bowl. Weigh the pulp. Return it to the pan with the spices.
3. Add the required amount of sugar to the pulp and heat gently, stirring until the sugar has dissolved completely. Bring to a boil and boil steadily until very thick and creamy, stirring frequently.
4. Remove the pan from the heat. Pour into warmed, sterilized jars, cover with waxed discs and leave until cold before sealing tightly with lids.

Blackberry Butter

Wild blackberries are at their best when plump, ripe, and full of inky juice. Cultivated blackberries lack the deep flavor of wild berries, but they are nevertheless still delicious and have the advantage of having fewer seeds than the wild variety. They make a beautiful amethyst-colored spread that is delicious with scones and cream or as a filling for a plain sponge cake.

TOTAL TIME: 1 HOUR | MAKES: ABOUT TWO 16-OZ (500 ML) JARS PER 1 LB (450 G) SUGAR

- 36 oz (1 kg) blackberries
- 2 lbs 3 oz (1 kg) cooking apples, coarsely chopped including cores and peel
- Grated zest and juice of 2 lemons
- 12 oz (350 g) granulated or superfine sugar to every 1 lb (450 g) fruit pulp (see step 2)

1. Put the blackberries and apples (including cores and peel) into a large, heavy-based pan with the lemon zest and juice. Slowly bring to a boil. Reduce the heat and simmer gently for about 15 minutes until very soft.

2. Remove the pan from the heat. Push through a sieve and weigh the pulp. Stir in the required amount of sugar, and heat gently until the sugar has dissolved completely.

3. Bring to a boil and cook steadily for about 20 minutes until the mixture is thick and creamy, stirring the whole time. The actual cooking time will depend on the ripeness of the fruit.

4. Remove the pan from the heat. Pour into warmed, sterilized jars and cover with plastic or metal lids. Label and store in a cool place, and use within a month.

PLUM BUTTER

You can use any type of plum for this recipe, such as damsons or greengages. Plums come in dozens of varieties, shapes, sizes, and colors. Whether green, red, deep purple, or almost black, they are delicious eaten fresh or baked in puddings, pies, cakes, and jams. The plum is closely related to the almond, cherry, peach, and other species of the genus *Prunus*.

TOTAL TIME: 1 HOUR 40 MINUTES | MAKES: ABOUT TWO 16-OZ (500 ML) JARS PER 1 LB (450 G) SUGAR

- 3 lbs 5 oz (1.5 kg) ripe plums
- Water (see step 1)
- 12 oz (350 g) granulated or superfine sugar to every 1 lb (450 g) fruit pulp (see step 2)

1. Remove the pits from the plums and put into a large, heavy-based pan with just enough water to cover the fruit. Simmer gently for about 20 minutes, or until very soft.
2. Remove the pan from the heat. Push through a sieve into a bowl. Weigh the pulp and return it to the pan. Add the required amount of sugar. Heat gently, stirring until the sugar has dissolved completely.
3. Bring to a boil and cook gently for about 40–60 minutes until very thick, stirring frequently.
4. Remove the pan from the heat. Pour into warmed, sterilized jars, cover with waxed discs, and leave until cold before sealing tightly with lids.

QUINCE BUTTER

Quinces can be found in specialty food stores and some large supermarkets in the autumn. This preserve is delicious with cheese and crackers, bread and butter, or roast pork. Wash the quinces and scrub off the gray down before you start.

TOTAL TIME: 1 HOUR 40 MINUTES | MAKES: ABOUT TWO 16-OZ (500 ML) JARS PER 1 LB (450 G) SUGAR

- 2 lbs 3 oz (1 kg) quinces (peeled and cored weight)
- 1¾ cups (450 mL) water
- 1 lb (450 g) granulated or superfine sugar to every 1 lb (450 g) fruit pulp (see step 2)
- 3 Tbsp (44 mL) lemon juice to every 1 lb (450 g) fruit pulp (see step 2)
- 2 Tbsp (28 g) unsalted butter

1. Cut the quinces into small pieces and place in a large, heavy-based pan with the water. Bring to a boil, then reduce the heat. Simmer gently for about 20–40 minutes, or until very soft.

2. Remove the pan from the heat. Push through a sieve into a bowl. Weigh the pulp and return it to the pan. Add the required amount of sugar and lemon juice. Heat gently, stirring until the sugar has dissolved completely. Bring to a boil and cook gently for about 40 minutes until very thick, stirring frequently.

3. Remove the pan from the heat. Pour into warmed, sterilized jars, cover with waxed discs, and cover with plastic or metal lids immediately.

APRICOT CURD

Fresh, golden, juicy apricots can vary in color from pale yellow to deep orange. They make a delectable spread for fresh bread and butter, as well as scones. Add a few of the cracked pits to the mixture for a subtle almond flavor, but remember to remove them before potting.

TOTAL TIME: 1 HOUR | MAKES: ABOUT THREE 4-OZ (125 ML) JARS

- 8 oz (225 g) fresh ripe apricots, cut in half
- 8 oz (225 g) granulated or superfine sugar
- Grated zest and juice of 1 lemon
- 4 Tbsp (50 g) unsalted butter, diced
- 2 eggs, beaten

1. Put the apricots into a medium pan with very little water, and cook for about 15–20 minutes until soft. Push the mixture through a nylon sieve into a heatproof bowl. Stir in the sugar, lemon zest, lemon juice, and butter.
2. Place the bowl over a pan of simmering (but not boiling) water and cook, stirring until the sugar has dissolved.
3. Stir in the eggs. Continue stirring for about 20 minutes until the mixture thickens enough to coat the back of a wooden spoon. Be careful not to cook for too long as the mixture will thicken more as it cools.
4. Remove the bowl and pan from the heat. Pour into warmed, sterilized jars, cover with waxed discs, and leave until cold before sealing tightly with cellophane covers or lids.
5. Label and store in a cool place, and use within a month.

GOOSEBERRY CURD

Hard, bright-green gooseberries are one of the first fruits of the year. They are sharp and sour tasting when raw, but their acidity is transformed by cooking them with sugar. In wet weather, gooseberries exude more liquid so may need cooking for a little longer.

TOTAL TIME: 1 HOUR 5 MINUTES | MAKES: ABOUT ONE 32-OZ (1 L) JAR

- 16 oz (450 g) green gooseberries
- 2 Tbsp (30 mL) water
- 4 oz (110 g) unsalted butter
- 8 oz (225 g) granulated or superfine sugar
- 3 large eggs

1. Put the gooseberries (there's no need to top and tail them) into a large, heavy-based pan with the water. Bring to a boil and simmer gently for about 15 minutes until very soft.

2. Remove the pan from the heat. Push the mixture through a sieve into a bowl and reserve.

3. Put the butter and sugar into a separate, large, heatproof bowl; place over a pan of simmering (but not boiling) water; and stir to dissolve the sugar. When the butter has melted and the sugar has dissolved completely, stir in the reserved gooseberry purée.

4. Beat the eggs lightly and stir into the warm mixture. Cook over the simmering water for about 20–30 minutes, stirring until the mixture thickens enough to coat the back of a spoon.

5. Remove the bowl and pan from the heat. Pour into warmed, sterilized jars, cover with waxed discs, and leave until cold before sealing tightly with lids.

LEMON CURD

This tastes so much nicer than the commercial variety and has a lovely fresh-lemon flavor with just a hint of sharpness. Some lemons may be waxed to protect them from bruising during shipping. As zest is used in this recipe, it is best to use organically grown lemons and limes, which are unwaxed. Alternatively, scrub the fruit very well in warm water to remove the waxy coating.

TOTAL TIME: 30 MINUTES | MAKES: ABOUT THREE 4-OZ (125 ML) JARS

- Finely grated zest and juice of 2 large lemons
- 8 oz (225 g) granulated or superfine sugar
- 4 oz (110 g) unsalted butter, diced
- 2 large eggs, lightly beaten

1. Put the lemon zest, juice, sugar, and butter into a heatproof bowl. Place over a pan of simmering (but not boiling) water, and stir to dissolve the sugar.
2. Stir in the eggs and continue stirring for about 20 minutes until the mixture thickens enough to coat the back of a wooden spoon. Be careful not to cook for too long, as the mixture will thicken more as it cools.
3. Remove the bowl and pan from the heat. Pour into warmed, sterilized jars, cover with waxed discs, and leave until cold before sealing tightly with cellophane covers or lids.
4. Store in a cool place and use within a month.

PUMPKIN CURD

The onset of autumn brings with it the annual appearance of a colorful array of pumpkins ranging in color from pale gold to deep, dark green. This curd makes an unusual filling for a sponge cake and is also good spread on scones and bread.

TOTAL TIME: 1 HOUR 15 MINUTES | MAKES: ABOUT ONE 32-OZ (1 L) JAR

- 1 lb (450 g) pumpkin (peeled and seeded weight)
- 2 large eggs
- 1 lb (450 g) granulated or superfine sugar
- Juice of 2 large lemons

1. Cut the pumpkin flesh into pieces, and put them into a large sieve or metal colander over a pan of boiling water. Cover and steam for 30 minutes, then mash to a purée. Transfer to a heatproof bowl.
2. Beat the eggs lightly and stir into the warm purée with the sugar and lemon juice.
3. Cook over a pan of simmering (but not boiling) water for about 20–30 minutes, stirring until the mixture thickens enough to coat the back of a spoon.
4. Remove the bowl and pan from the heat. Pour into warmed, sterilized jars, cover with waxed discs, and leave until cold before sealing tightly with lids

DAMSON CHEESE

Damsons are indigestible when raw, but this fruit is transformed during cooking and makes wonderful preserves. Serve this preserve sliced with roast lamb or beef, or as a dessert with whipped cream.

TOTAL TIME: 2 HOURS | MAKES: ABOUT THREE 8-OZ (250 ML) JARS PER 1 LB (450 G) SUGAR

- 3 lbs (1.3 kg) damsons
- ⅔–1 cup (150–250 mL) water
- 1 lb (450 g) granulated or superfine sugar for each 1 lb (450 g) fruit pulp (see steps 2 and 4)

1. Put the whole damsons into a large, heavy-based pan with the water. Bring to a boil and simmer gently for about 30 minutes until very soft.
2. Push the mixture through a sieve into a bowl. Weigh the pulp and return it to the pan.

3. Crack the damson pits and remove the kernels. Chop these finely and add to the pulp to give a strong almond flavor to the finished cheese. If you prefer, you can use just half the kernels or omit them altogether.
4. Add the required amount of sugar to the pulp and heat gently, stirring until the sugar has dissolved completely. Bring to a boil and cook gently for about 1 hour or until very thick, stirring frequently.

5. Remove the bowl and pan from the heat. Pour into warmed, sterilized jars, cover with waxed discs, and leave until cold before sealing tightly with lids.

Chutney

Chutney is a piquantly sweet-sour condiment made from fruits and vegetables and may range from mildly spiced to very hot. Chutney will pep up bland foods into a tasty meal (add a spoonful to a baked potato, for instance). It keeps very well, and the flavor actually improves if the chutney is left for at least two months before opening the jar.

Adding chutney to many dishes changes the flavor immensely.

Kilner jars have a double-locking system, where a metal disc and a screw top are both used to properly seal.

Equipment

- Use **a stainless steel or anodized aluminum pan**—never brass, copper, old-fashioned aluminum, or iron—as vinegar will react with and corrode these metals and also taint the chutney.
- **A wide funnel** is useful when filling the jars, but a jug or a small ladle can be used instead.
- **Kilner or Mason jars** are ideal for storing homemade preserves and come in a range of sizes. A Kilner jar is a glass jar that has a lid in two sections to ensure an airtight seal. A metal disc sits on top of the jar, and it is secured in place with a metal screw band containing a rubber seal. Another widely available glass jar has a rubber seal and a metal hinge, which forms an airtight seal when closed.
- **Lids** must be vinegar-proof, as in, lined with plastic. Plastic lids from coffee jars are perfect. Cellophane covers are not suitable—lids must also be completely airtight or the chutney will dry out as the vinegar evaporates. If you only have metal lids, line them with a disc of wax paper first.

Ingredients

Choose fresh-looking, firm, ripe fruits and vegetables. Fruits and vegetables are usually finely chopped or minced. Dried fruits are often included to add sweetness.

- **Currants, raisins and sultanas** all come from different types of grapes. Muscatel raisins are the finest raisin option, as they are plump and full of rich sweet flavor; however, they are more expensive. Sultanas are dried white grapes, paler than currants and raisins.
- **Prunes** are dried plums, and these glistening black fruits have a splendid flavor and moist texture. Some fruits, such as prunes and apricots, need soaking before use, although no-soak varieties are now widely available. You can use either in the recipes, but if using fruits that require soaking, you can make these even more delicious by soaking in orange juice, apple juice, wine, or tea, instead of water.
- **Dried dates** come from the fruit of a palm tree and have a rich sweet flavor.
- **Dried figs** are another great option. They flourish in hot countries, and in the past,

Sultanas are dried white grapes, paler than currants and raisins.

cooked figs were used as sweeteners in place of expensive sugar and are still used for this purpose today in North Africa and the Middle East. The best are Smyrna figs, which have a whitish coating of crystallized natural sugars.

- The best **dried apricots** are those from the Hunza Valley in Kashmir, Afghanistan, and Turkey. The wild fruits are left on the trees to dry before they are picked. Hunza apricots look uninviting: small, round, hard and beige in color, looking like little pits, totally unlike fresh, plump, vivid orange apricots. They need to be soaked and cooked before cooking, but their flavor is unsurpassable—deep and rich with a hint of toffee.

- **Cranberries, blueberries, and a variety of exotic fruits** such as papaya and mango are newcomers to the dried fruit market. These don't need to be soaked before use and are used in the same way as currants, raisins, etc.

- **Vinegar** is a key ingredient as it acts as a preservative and contributes to the flavor. It is important to use good-quality vinegar with an acetic acid content of at least 5%; never use anything labeled "nonbrewed condiment." The type of vinegar you use will give a different flavor to the chutney. Color is not an indication of strength; malt vinegar—whether white, distilled, or brown—is the least expensive and strongest tasting. Brown malt vinegar is used for making rich dark chutneys, while white malt vinegar is better for lighter chutneys, so the pale color is not spoiled. Cider vinegar is golden with a delicate flavor best suited to fruit chutneys. Wine vinegar can be either red or white, and red has the stronger flavor. It is not as harsh as malt vinegar and requires less time to soften the chutney after potting.

- **Sugar** may be white or brown, and the latter will give a darker color and stronger flavor. Black treacle is sometimes included to give extra flavor.

- **Spices** are an important ingredient and are included to give the chutney the necessary savory spicy flavor. They should be as fresh as possible. Using old, stale spices that have been

Different types of vinegar can be used for a variety of chutneys.

in the cupboard for a long time won't flavor the chutney at all, so make sure they are freshly bought. Spices can be whole or ground. Whole spices give a better flavor, as the volatile oils are preserved during storage. These should be bruised (beaten lightly with a rolling pin or other heavy object) to release their flavor, then tied in a piece of muslin so they can be removed easily before potting.

POPULAR SPICES FOR CHUTNEY AND PICKLES

- **Allspice** is not a blend of spices as many people wrongly think but is a spice in its own right. It has a highly aromatic flavor, often described as a combination of cinnamon, clove, nutmeg, and pepper. Allspice is available ground or as whole dried berries.
- **Cardamom** is the dried, unopened fruit of a plant native to south India. It has a warm, spicy, sweet, slightly lemony flavor and is sold whole in pods, as small blackish brown seeds, and ground. The pods and seeds should be lightly crushed before using to release the flavor.
- **Cayenne pepper** is a red, fiery hot spice ground from the pod and seeds of dried chilies and should be used sparingly. Just a pinch is all that's usually required.
- **Cinnamon** has a warm, sweet fragrance and is sold as sticks and as a powder. You can try to grind your own cinnamon from the bark, but it's difficult to get it fine enough. It's best to buy ground cinnamon in small quantities because the freshness and flavor quickly disappear.
- **Cloves** are the dried flower buds of a tree in Indonesia. Cloves have a pungent, spicy flavor and should be used sparingly.

A collection of spices is a must for an avid chutney maker.

- **Coriander** has a warm, aromatic, slightly nutty flavor with a hint of orange and is sold ground or whole as seeds.
- **Cumin** is sold as whole seeds or ground, and it imparts a warm, slightly sweet spiciness to chutneys.
- **Ginger** can be used as the fresh root, crystallized or candied in syrup, or dried and ground. It adds a touch of heat and has a warm fragrant aroma and flavor.
- **Juniper berries** have a bittersweet, slightly resinous flavor and should be lightly crushed or bruised before using to release the volatile flavoring oils.
- **Mace** is the outer lacy covering of the nutmeg. It is sold either in blades or ground, and it adds a mild nutmeg flavor.

- **Mustard seed** has a fresh clean fresh aroma and pungent, sharp flavor.
- **Nutmeg** has a warm, spicy flavor. Buy whole nutmeg and grate it as you need it. Avoid using ready-ground nutmeg, which quickly loses its flavor.
- **Pumpkin pie spice** is a commercial blend of sweet spices, including cinnamon, nutmeg, cloves, and ginger. It adds a warm spicy note.
- **Turmeric** is the root or rhizome of a member of the ginger family. It adds a pungent flavor and deep orange-yellow color. It is sold ground.

Cooking

It's a good idea to open the kitchen windows and close the kitchen door, or the pungent smell of boiling vinegar will permeate throughout the house.

Chutney is cooked slowly for a long time to give a good, rich flavor and dark color. The mixture is stirred with a wooden spoon from time to time to prevent it from sticking to the pan and burning. After cooking for about an hour, the chutney will need constant stirring. It should have a spoonable consistency, but it will also thicken a little more as it cools. Depending on the recipe, the mixture will need cooking for one to three hours, but be careful not to cook it for too long or the sugar will caramelize.

The texture may be chunky or smooth, depending on the recipe. Chutneys do not set with pectin; it is the evaporation of the vinegar that results in the correct texture, as chutneys will set firmer when cold. To test when the chutney is cooked, make a channel across the surface with a wooden spoon: if the impression lasts for a few seconds and does not fill up with vinegar, it is ready. Taste the chutney but remember that chutney needs time in the jar to mellow, allowing the acidity to soften and the flavors to develop.

The hot chutney is poured into warmed, sterilized jars right up to the brim and covered while still hot. Chutney will taste better if left to mature for at least three months before eating and will keep in a cool, dry, dark place for two to three years. Once opened, store in the refrigerator.

! WHAT CAN GO WRONG?

Raw flavor is caused by not cooking the mixture sufficiently. The longer chutney is cooked, the richer and mellower the flavor will be.

APPLE, APRICOT, AND CARDAMOM CHUTNEY

This combination of flavor is particularly delicious with pork, ham, or sausages. Cardamom seeds are very fragrant and impart a highly aromatic, warm, citrus-like flavor with subtle floral tones. Light muscovado sugar adds a rich taste with a hint of molasses.

TOTAL TIME: 1 HOUR 30 MINUTES | MAKES: ABOUT TWO 32-OZ (1 L) JARS

- 1 lb (450 g) onions, peeled and finely chopped
- 1¼ cups (300 mL) white malt vinegar
- 2 lbs 3 oz (1 kg) cooking apples (peeled and cored weight)
- 2 tsp cardamom seeds, crushed
- 12 oz (350 g) light muscovado sugar
- 4 oz (110 g) dried apricots, roughly chopped
- Salt and pepper, to taste

1. Put the onions and half the vinegar into a large, heavy-based pan and bring to a boil. Reduce the heat and simmer gently for 10 minutes
2. Cut the apples into small pieces, and add to the pan with the remaining vinegar, cardamom seeds, sugar, dried apricots, and a sprinkling of salt and pepper.
3. Stir over a low heat until the sugar has dissolved completely. Increase the heat and simmer steadily for about 40–60 minutes, stirring occasionally until the mixture is very thick.
4. Remove the pan from the heat. Spoon into hot sterilized jars, seal, and label.
5. Leave to mature for up to three months in a cool, dry, dark place.

APRICOT AND ONION CHUTNEY

Dried apricots have a more pronounced flavor than fresh ones, but either option can be used. This is a mild-tasting chutney that goes well with all kinds of meat, poultry, pies, as well as cheese.

TOTAL TIME: 1 HOUR 15 MINUTES | MAKES: ABOUT TWO 32-OZ (1 L) JARS

- 8 oz (225 g) apricots
- 1 large onion, peeled
- 1 lb (450 g) cooking apples (peeled and cored weight)
- 1 tsp salt
- 4 oz (110 g) sultanas
- 2½ cups (600 mL) vinegar
- 1 lb (450 g) light muscovado sugar

1. Put all the ingredients, except the sugar, into a large, heavy-based pan and bring to a boil. Reduce the heat and simmer for about 45 minutes until the mixture is thick and pulpy. Remove from the heat and stir in the sugar until completely dissolved.

2. Return to a low heat and stir well. Increase the heat and simmer steadily for about 20 minutes, stirring occasionally until the mixture is very thick.

3. Remove the pan from the heat. Spoon into hot sterilized jars, seal, and label.

AUTUMN CHUTNEY

This recipe is an ideal way to use up a glut of autumn fruits. Vary the proportions of fruit according to what you have available, as long as the total weight of fruit remains the same. For example, you could use blackberries instead of the apricots, or use half the amount of pears and make up the weight with plums.

TOTAL TIME: 1 HOUR 25 MINUTES | MAKES: ABOUT SEVEN 8-OZ (250 ML) JARS

- 1 lb (450 g) onions, peeled and finely chopped
- 1¼ cups (300 mL) white malt vinegar
- 1 lb (450 g) cooking apples (peeled and cored weight)
- 1 lb (450 g) pears (peeled and cored weight)
- 4 oz (110 g) dried apricots, chopped
- 12 oz (350 g) light muscovado sugar
- Salt and pepper, to taste

1. Put the onions and half the vinegar into a large, heavy-based pan and bring to a boil. Reduce the heat and simmer gently for 10 minutes.
2. Cut the apples and pears into small pieces, and add to the pan with the remaining vinegar, apricots, sugar, and a sprinkling of salt and pepper.
3. Stir over a low heat until the sugar has dissolved completely. Increase the heat and simmer steadily for about 40–60 minutes, stirring occasionally until the mixture is very thick.
4. Remove the pan from the heat. Spoon into hot sterilized jars, seal, and label.
5. Leave to mature for at least 3 months in a cool, dry, dark place.

BEETROOT CHUTNEY

Beetroot has a wonderful color, and when combined with onions and apples, makes for a tasty chutney that's ideal with cheese and cold meats. It is also good with poultry.

TOTAL TIME: 1 HOUR 15 MINUTES | MAKES: ABOUT TWO 32-OZ (1 L) JARS

- 5 cups (1 kg) raw and peeled beetroot, grated or shredded
- 1 lb (450 g) onions, peeled and chopped
- 1 lb 8 oz (680 g) apples, peeled and chopped
- 16 oz (450 g) seedless raisins
- 4½ cups (1.1 L) malt vinegar
- 1 tsp mixed pickling spices
- 5 cups (1 kg) white or brown sugar

1. Put all the ingredients in a large, heavy-based pan and slowly bring to a boil. Reduce the heat and simmer gently for about 1 hour until soft and pulpy.
2. Remove the pan from the heat. Spoon into hot sterilized jars, seal, and label.

ELDERBERRY CHUTNEY

A tasty chutney with a fruity flavor. Glossy, black elderberries are the fruit of the elder tree and can be found growing wild in the autumn. They must never be eaten raw as the uncooked berries can cause nausea or vomiting and so are always cooked. The easiest way to remove the berries from the stalks is to strip them using the prongs of a fork.

TOTAL TIME: 2 HOURS | MAKES: ABOUT SEVEN 8-OZ (250 ML) JARS

- 16 oz (450 g) elderberries, washed and stalks removed
- 1 lb (450 g) cooking apples, peeled, cored, and chopped
- 4 oz (110 g) dried fruit, such as a mix of currants, sultanas, and raisins
- 1 lb (450 g) onions, peeled and finely chopped
- 1 tsp salt
- ½ tsp ground ginger
- ½ tsp pumpkin pie spice
- Pinch of ground black pepper

- 1¼ cups (300 mL) malt vinegar
- 12 oz (350 g) white or brown sugar

1. Put the elderberries, apples, dried fruit, and onions into a large heavy based pan with the salt, spices, pepper, and one third of the vinegar. Bring to a boil. Reduce the heat and simmer very gently for about 1 hour until the fruit is soft, stirring from time to time to prevent the mixture sticking and burning.

2. Remove from the heat and stir in the sugar and remaining vinegar. When the sugar has dissolved completely, return to the heat and bring to a boil. Boil steadily for about 30–40 minutes until thick.

3. Remove the pan from the heat. Spoon into hot sterilized jars, seal, and label.

GOOSEBERRY CHUTNEY

A well-flavored, fruity, spicy chutney that's delicious with rich, oily fish, particularly mackerel and smoked salmon. It is also a tasty accompaniment to roast meats and poultry. Cayenne pepper adds a hot spiciness, and you can use more or less as you prefer.

TOTAL TIME: 2 HOURS 10 MINUTES | MAKES: ABOUT TWO 32-OZ (1 L) JARS

- 53 oz (1.5 kg) green gooseberries, topped and tailed
- 1 lb (450 g) onions, peeled and finely chopped
- 8 oz (225 g) seedless raisins
- 1 Tbsp (18 g) salt
- 1 tsp ground ginger
- ½ tsp cayenne pepper
- 12 oz (350 g) soft brown sugar
- 2½ cups (600 mL) white vinegar

1. Put all the ingredients in a large, heavy-based pan over a low heat. Slowly bring to a boil, stirring until the sugar has dissolved completely.
2. Reduce the heat and simmer gently, for about 1–2 hours, stirring frequently until thick.
3. Remove the pan from the heat. Spoon into hot sterilized jars, seal, and label.

GREEN TOMATO CHUTNEY

Green tomatoes have a firm texture and a sharp flavor with just a hint of tomato. This is a recipe that was popular with the Victorians, who regarded this as an ideal accompaniment to cheeses and cold meats.

TOTAL TIME: 1 HOUR 40 MINUTES | MAKES: ABOUT TWO 32-OZ (1 L) JARS

- 3 lbs 5 oz (1.5 kg) green tomatoes, sliced
- 1 lb (450 g) cooking apples, peeled, cored, and chopped
- 1 lb 8 oz (680 g) shallots or onions, peeled and finely chopped
- 2 cloves garlic, peeled (optional)
- 8 oz (225 g) raisins
- 1 tsp salt
- ½ tsp cayenne pepper
- ½ oz (15 g) fresh root ginger, bruised
- 2½ cups (600 mL) vinegar
- 1 lb (450 g) soft brown sugar

1. Put the tomatoes, apples, shallots, garlic, and raisins in a large, heavy-based pan with the salt and cayenne pepper. Tie the ginger loosely in a piece of muslin and add to the pan.

2. Stir in one third of the vinegar, and cook gently over a low heat for about 1 hour until the vegetables and fruit are soft, stirring from time to time.

3. Remove from the heat and stir in the sugar and remaining vinegar. When the sugar has dissolved completely, return to the heat and bring to a boil. Reduce the heat and simmer gently for 1–1½ hours until thick.

4. Remove the pan from the heat. Spoon into hot sterilized jars, seal, and label.

PEAR AND ORANGE CHUTNEY

There are over 5,000 varieties of pears and any can be used in this recipe, although slightly underripe pears are best for cooking. Oranges add a refreshing, sweet tartness to this chutney. It is particularly good with duck and other rich-tasting meats.

TOTAL TIME: 2 HOURS 25 MINUTES | MAKES: ABOUT TWO 32-OZ (1 L) JARS

- 3 lbs 5 oz (1.5 kg) hard pears (peeled and cored weight), roughly chopped
- 1 large onion, peeled and finely chopped
- 8 oz (225 g) seedless raisins
- 12 oz (350 g) light muscovado sugar
- Finely grated zest and juice of 2 oranges
- 1 tsp ground ginger
- Pinch of ground cloves

1. Put all the ingredients into a large, heavy-based pan.
2. Stir well over a low heat until the sugar has dissolved completely. Bring to a boil then reduce the heat and simmer gently for 1–2 hours, stirring occasionally until thick.
3. Remove the pan from the heat. Spoon into hot sterilized jars, seal, and label.

RHUBARB CHUTNEY

Young succulent stems of rhubarb have a refreshingly tart flavor. This tasty chutney is excellent with fatty meats, such as pork or duck, when its sharp, fresh taste will cut through the richness of the meat.

TOTAL TIME: 2 HOURS 30 MINUTES | MAKES: ABOUT TWO 32-OZ (1 L) JARS

- ⅔ cup (150 mL) water
- ⅔ cup (150 mL) vinegar
- 5 cups (1 kg) white or brown sugar
- 1 tsp ground allspice
- 1 tsp ground ginger
- ½ tsp ground cloves
- 3 lbs 5 oz (1.5 kg) rhubarb, cut into 1" (2.5 cm) pieces
- 16 oz (450 g) sultanas or raisins

1. Put the water, vinegar, sugar, and spices into a large, heavy-based pan. Bring to a boil, then reduce the heat and simmer gently for 20 minutes.
2. Add the rhubarb and sultanas or raisins to the vinegar syrup, and bring to a boil. Reduce the heat and simmer gently for about 1–2 hours until thick.
3. Remove the pan from the heat. Spoon into hot sterilized jars, seal, and label.

RIPE TOMATO CHUTNEY

There are lots of varieties of tomatoes and any can be used to make this red chutney, which has a different flavor from chutney made with green tomatoes and looks and tastes very appetizing. To ripen homegrown tomatoes, place them in a paper bag with a ripe tomato and keep at room temperature.

TOTAL TIME: 1 HOUR | MAKES: ABOUT FIVE 16-OZ (500 ML) JARS

- 2 lbs 3 oz (1 kg) firm and ripe tomatoes, skinned and chopped
- 1 lb (450 g) onions, peeled and finely chopped
- 1 lb (450 g) cooking apples (peeled and cored weight), finely chopped
- 1¾ cups (450 mL) vinegar
- 1 tsp ground ginger
- 1 tsp pumpkin pie spice
- 12 oz (350 g) white or brown sugar
- 10½ oz (300 g) sultanas
- Salt and pepper, to taste

1. Put all the ingredients except the sugar, sultanas, salt, and pepper into a large, heavy-based pan. Bring to a boil, then reduce the heat and simmer steadily for about 20 minutes, stirring occasionally until thick.
2. Remove from the heat and stir in the sugar until dissolved completely. Add the sultanas and season to taste. Stir well, over a low heat. Increase the heat and simmer steadily for about 20 minutes, stirring occasionally until the mixture is very thick.
3. Remove the pan from the heat. Spoon into hot sterilized jars, seal, and label.

SPICY PINEAPPLE CHUTNEY

Fresh pineapple and spicy chili give this chutney a kick that's perfect with curries.

TOTAL TIME: 1 HOUR 15 MINUTES | MAKES: ABOUT ONE 32-OZ (1 L) JAR

- 2 Tbsp (30 mL) olive oil
- 2 onions, finely chopped
- 1 tsp mustard seeds, toasted
- ½ tsp ground turmeric
- ½ tsp ground ginger
- 1 clove garlic, finely chopped
- 1 red chili, chopped and seeds removed
- 1 pineapple, peeled, cored, and cut into chunks
- 1 sprig rosemary
- 1 Tbsp clear honey
- 7 Tbsp (100 mL) cider vinegar
- 4 oz (120 g) sugar
- Salt and pepper, to taste

1. Heat the oil in a frying pan. Cook the onions over a low heat until softened, but not browned.
2. Add the mustard seeds, spices, garlic, and chili and cook for 2 minutes.
3. Put into a large, heavy-based pan and add the remaining ingredients.
4. Stir over a low heat until the sugar has dissolved, then reduce the heat and simmer for 40–60 minutes until thick. Remove the rosemary. Season to taste with salt and pepper.
5. Spoon into hot, sterilized jars. Cover with vinegar-proof lids, seal, and label.

UNCOOKED CHUTNEY

An easy, simple recipe that is ready to eat as soon as it is made. It will keep for up to six weeks.

TOTAL TIME: 20 MINUTES | MAKES: ABOUT SEVEN 8-OZ (250 ML) JARS

- 8 oz (227 g) dates, finely chopped
- 8 oz (227 g) apples, peeled and chopped
- 8 oz (227 g) sultanas and raisins, mixed
- 8 oz (227 g) onion, finely chopped
- 8 oz (227 g) dark soft brown sugar
- 1¼ cups (300 mL) malt vinegar
- 1 tsp salt
- Pinch each of mustard powder and ground pepper
- ¼ tsp ground cinnamon
- Pinch of ground cloves

1. Mix all the ingredients together very well in a large bowl. Spoon into cold sterilized jars, filling to the brim.

2. Seal with vinegar-proof lids, label, and store in a cool, dry place.

Pickles and Fermented Foods

Piquant pickles add a kick to all sorts of food: cheeses, cold meats, poultry, meat pies, etc. A spoonful of pickle or a few crisp pickled onions are quick and tasty ways to spice up a plain meal or sandwich.

Pickling and fermenting foods is a great way to get additional nutrients out of your produce.

Stainless steel or anodized aluminum pans won't get corroded by vinegar.

Equipment

- Use **a stainless steel or anodized aluminum pan**—never brass, copper old-fashioned aluminum, or iron—as vinegar will react with and corrode these metals. Modern aluminum pans are anodized, a process that seals the metal, so are fine to use for pickles and chutneys.
- **Nylon sieves** are best, as metal could adversely affect the color and flavor of the finished pickles.
- **Kilner or Mason jars** are ideal for storing homemade preserves and come in a range of sizes. A Kilner jar is a glass jar that has a lid in two sections to ensure an airtight seal. A metal disc sits on top of the jar, and it is secured in place with a metal screw band containing a rubber seal. Another widely available glass jar has a rubber seal and a metal hinge, which forms an airtight seal when closed.
- **Lids** must be vinegar-proof, as in, lined with plastic. Plastic lids from coffee jars are perfect. If metal comes into contact with vinegar, the lids will rust. Lids must also be completely airtight, or the pickles will dry out as the vinegar evaporates. If you only have metal lids, line them with a disc of wax paper first. Cellophane covers are not suitable as they are too flimsy.

Ingredients

- **Vinegar** is a key ingredient as it acts as a preservative and contributes to the flavor. It is important to use good-quality vinegar with an acetic acid content of at least 5%; never use anything labeled "nonbrewed condiment." There are many types of vinegar; it can be made from grapes, grains, or fruits, and each has its own subtly different flavor ranging from mild to strong. The type of vinegar you use will give a different flavor to the pickles.

You can pickle a wide variety of vegetables and store them for later—or eat them right away.

Color is not an indication of strength; malt vinegar—whether white, distilled, or brown—is the least expensive and strongest tasting. Brown malt vinegar is used for making dark pickles. White malt vinegar is better for light and clear pickles so that the pale color is not spoiled. A commercially made spiced "pickling vinegar" is also available, which gives a spicy flavor to the finished pickles.

- **Cider vinegar**, golden with a delicate flavor, or wine vinegar can also be used, although these are more expensive. White wine vinegar, cider vinegar, or white malt vinegar is the best to use for pickled fruits, so that the color is not impaired.
- **Pickling salt or sea salt** is the best to use for brining rather than table salt as the latter has additives, which tend to make the brine cloudy.
- **Spices** (page 74) are essential to add an interesting and subtle flavor to the pickles. Pickling spice mixes are available, and the blends differ greatly according to the manufacturer. The spices usually include allspice, bay leaves, cardamom, cinnamon, cloves, coriander, ginger, mustard seeds, and peppercorns and are usually whole or in large pieces. Whole spices give a better flavor, as the volatile oils are preserved

Sea salt is preferred over table salt.

during storage. Use spices sparingly, as they can be overpowering.

- **Sugar**, whether you prefer white or brown, is added to the vinegar and spices to make sweet pickles. These have a sharp but not sour flavor and are excellent with cold meats and poultry.
- **Fruits and vegetables**, such as plums, blackberries, onions, and beetroot, can be pickled. Spices can be added to vary the flavor. Herb sprigs or leaves also add flavor. Bay leaves have a strong aromatic flavor and exude a wonderful aroma when crushed.

White or brown sugar can be used for pickling and fermenting.

POPULAR VEGETABLES FOR PICKLING

- **Cucumbers** for pickling should be young and measure between 2"–4" (5–10 cm), which makes them easier to fit in the jar. Prick them once or twice to allow the flavors to penetrate better.

- **Mushrooms** should be firm and fresh looking with no sign of sweating, and the stalk end should be moist, not dry. Small mushrooms, such as button mushrooms, are the best to use. Wild mushrooms are excellent, but unless you know what you are doing, don't be tempted to pick wild mushrooms; **some deadly poisonous mushrooms look remarkably similar to edible varieties**! Wild mushrooms are becoming more easily available from specialist shops and local markets, and their flavor is far superior to that of cultivated varieties, with each variety having its own very unique flavor.

- **Onions** are probably the most popular vegetable for pickling. The two most commonly used are shallots and pickling or baby onions, which will fit easily into jars. Choose firm onions with unbroken skins; shallots should not have too much evident growth shoot, as this indicates that they are past their best.

Red cabbage is perfect for sauerkraut.

- **Red cabbage** is a favorite for pickling and should have a tight, compact head that feels heavy for its size. It should look crisp and fresh with few loose leaves. Discard any outer limp leaves. Remove the core and discard. Shred the cabbage just before you plan to use it to preserve the vitamin C.

Only fresh mushrooms should be used for pickling.

Preparation and Cooking

Some vegetables need blanching before pickling, others need no cooking, and some are cooked in the vinegar as part of the pickling process. The vegetables are immersed in a wet or dry brine for a specified time, then drained and rinsed thoroughly under cold running water. The purpose of this is to extract some of the moisture from the vegetables (which otherwise would dilute the vinegar and reduce its preserving quality), keep them firm and crisp, and add to the clarity of the pickles. Each vegetable is treated differently according to type, so follow the instructions in individual recipes.

After rinsing, the vegetables are packed into jars, so they don't become squashed or bruised. The jars are filled with spiced vinegar almost to the top. Leave a ½" (1.3cm) space between the vinegar and the top of the jar. Cold vinegar produces crisp sharp pickles; alternatively, the vinegar can also be heated before pouring into the jars, which produces softer pickles.

Sweet pickles are made by simmering the fruits or vegetables with vinegar, sugar, and spices. After potting, the vinegar syrup is boiled down until reduced, then poured over the fruits into the jars. Shake the jars occasionally during storage to distribute the fruit and syrup evenly. Be careful not to overcook the fruit in sweet pickles, as it should retain a firm texture.

Pickles must be stored in a cool, dark, dry place to prevent discoloration. They are best left for at least one month before using. Once opened, store in the refrigerator.

 WHAT CAN GO WRONG?

Soft fruits or vegetables, which have lost their crisp texture, are due to being stored for too long. Pickles will retain their crisp texture for up to a year if stored correctly.

CHOW CHOW

This tangy relish is a common everyday side at many Amish meals and is sometimes referred to as "end-of-the-season" relish.

TOTAL TIME: 40 MINUTES, PLUS STANDING OVERNIGHT | MAKES: ABOUT ONE 16-OZ (500 ML) JAR

- 6 oz (175 g) chopped peppers
- 3 oz (90 g) chopped cabbage
- 1 cucumber, chopped
- 5 oz (150 g) chopped onion
- 7½ cups (1.8 L) water
- 3 Tbsp (55 g) salt
- 4½ oz (125 g) chopped carrots
- 4½ oz (125 g) chopped green beans
- 2 tsp mustard seeds
- 2 tsp celery seeds
- 2 cups (450 mL) vinegar
- 1 lb (450 g) sugar

1. Soak the peppers, cabbage, cucumber, and onion in the water and salt overnight. Drain well.
2. Cook the carrots and green beans in boiling water for 10 minutes and drain well.
3. Mix together all the ingredients in a large pan and bring to a boil.
4. Pack into hot sterilized jars. Seal with vinegar-proof lids and label.

CUCUMBER PICKLE

This sweet pickle is also known as bread and butter pickle, as it is delicious eaten with thickly sliced bread and butter. It is also good with cold meats and cheese.

TOTAL TIME: 35 MINUTES, PLUS 3 HOURS STANDING | MAKES: ABOUT TWO 32-OZ (1 L) JARS

- 3 large cucumbers, thinly sliced
- 2 large onions, peeled and thinly sliced
- 8 tsp (50 g) salt
- 2½ cups (600 mL) cider or white distilled vinegar
- 1 lb (450 g) granulated or superfine sugar
- ½ tsp ground turmeric
- 1 tsp celery seed
- 1 tsp mustard seed

1. Arrange the cucumber and onion slices in alternate layers in a large bowl, sprinkling salt between each layer. Cover with a weighted plate and leave to stand for at least 3 hours. Drain off the salty liquid, and rinse and dry the vegetables well.

2. Put the cider or vinegar, sugar, and spices into a large, heavy-based pan, and stir over a low heat until the sugar has dissolved completely.

3. Add the cucumber and onion to the mixture, and bring to a boil. Boil for 1 minute, then remove from the heat. Remove the vegetables and mustard seeds with a slotted spoon and pack into jars.

4. Boil the vinegar syrup for about 10 minutes until reduced, then remove from the heat and pour over the vegetables to completely cover them. Cover, seal, and label when cold.

GRANDMA HANNAH'S
READY-TO-EAT PICKLES

A treasured Amish recipe that's very tasty.

TOTAL TIME: 25 MINUTES, PLUS 30 MINUTES STANDING | MAKES: ABOUT ONE 16-OZ (500 ML) JAR

- 2 lbs 3 oz (1 kg) cucumbers, thinly sliced
- 1 Tbsp (18 g) celery seeds
- 1 Tbsp (18 g) salt
- 1 onion, sliced
- 1 pepper, sliced
- 1 lb (450 g) sugar
- 1 cup (225 mL) vinegar

1. Sprinkle the cucumber slices with celery seeds and salt, and leave to stand for 30 minutes. Drain well and put into a bowl with the onions and peppers.
2. Mix together the sugar and vinegar until the sugar is dissolved (do not heat). Pour over the vegetables and mix well.
3. Pickles can be eaten immediately or stored in the refrigerator.

KIMCHI

Kimchi, the Korean national dish, has a tangy, spicy flavor and has been prized for hundreds of years in East Asia. It's packed with vitamins, minerals, and beneficial natural probiotic bacteria and is associated with many health benefits.

Filtered water is needed for this recipe because tap water often contains a small amount of chlorine, which will inhibit the fermentation process. Use either a filter pitcher or bottled water. Use Korean gochugaru chili flakes if possible; it will give an authentic flavor and is available online and in Chinese or Korean supermarkets.

TOTAL TIME: 45 MINUTES, PLUS 8 HOURS STANDING | MAKES: ABOUT ONE 16-OZ (500 ML) JAR

- 1 large napa cabbage (Chinese cabbage)
- 2 Tbsp (40 g) sea salt
- 32 oz (1 L) filtered water
- 4 garlic cloves, peeled
- 2 Tbsp (12 g) freshly grated ginger
- 1–3 red chilies, depending on how hot you want it
- 1 mooli (Chinese radish), cut into ⅛" (3 mm) strips
- 5 spring onions, cut into ⅛" (3 mm) strips
- 1 medium carrot, cut into ⅛" (3 mm) strips
- 2 tsp gochujang or paprika (not smoked)

1. Put the cabbage in a large mixing bowl, and separate the leaves using your fingers. Arrange in layers, with salt sprinkled between each layer. Pour in the filtered water.
2. Cover the bowl with a tea towel and set aside for 8–12 hours or overnight—during this time the cabbage will take in beneficial yeasts and bacteria from the air.
3. Grind the garlic, ginger, and chili to a paste in a blender or pestle and mortar.
4. Drain the salted cabbage in a colander, and reserve the water. Return the cabbage to the bowl.
5. Add the mooli, spring onion, carrot, chili paste (step 3), and gochujang or paprika to the cabbage. Wearing rubber gloves to protect your hands from the chili, thoroughly massage the paste into the vegetables.
6. Pack the mixture into cold sterilized jars, pressing down tightly to ensure there are no air pockets. Pour in enough of the reserved salt water to come right to the top of the jars. Cover with the lid and seal securely.
7. Leave in a dark place at room temperature for 1–2 weeks to ferment. Check it daily to ensure it stays fully covered by the liquid. The longer you leave it, the more it will continue to ferment and become more fully flavored.

Mixed Pickles

A soft piquant pickle that goes well with cold meat and cheese.
The turmeric adds a warm, mildly spicy flavor and yellow color.

TOTAL TIME: 3 HOURS 20 MINUTES | MAKES: ABOUT NINE 8-OZ (250 ML) JARS

- 1 medium cucumber
- 1 lb (450 g) tomatoes, cut in half and seeds removed
- 1 lb 8 oz (680 g) zucchini or yellow squash, peeled and seeds removed
- 4⅔ cups (1.1 L) white vinegar
- 12 oz (350 g) demerara sugar
- 1 oz (25 g) salt
- ½ oz (15 g) ground turmeric
- 1 tsp pumpkin pie spice
- ¼ tsp ground mace

1. Mince or finely chop all the vegetables. A food processor makes short work of this. Put all the ingredients into a large, heavy-based pan, stir well and bring to a boil.
2. Reduce the heat and simmer gently for about 2–3 hours until thick and a dark color.
3. Remove from the heat. Pour into warmed, sterilized jars, then cover, seal, and label.

MOSTARDA DI FRUTTA (FRUIT MUSTARD)

A traditional sweet and spicy Italian condiment that's delicious with meats, poultry, and cheeses.

TOTAL TIME: 2 HOURS, 30 MINUTES | MAKES: ABOUT ONE 32-OZ (1 L) JAR

- 1 lb 10 oz (750 g) mixed fruit, e.g. figs, plums, pears, cherries, quince, apricots, etc.
- Water (see step 2)
- 1 lb (450 g) sugar
- Juice of ½ lemon
- ½ cup (120 mL) dry white wine
- 1¼ cups (300 mL) clear honey
- 3 Tbsp (55 g) mustard seeds
- 2 Tbsp (30 mL) English mustard

1. Peel the pears (if using) and chop the other fruits into small chunks, but leave the cherries whole.

2. Put all the fruit into a large pan and just cover with water. Add the sugar and lemon juice, and heat gently until the sugar has dissolved. Bring to a boil, reduce the heat and simmer for 10 minutes.

3. Heat the oven to its lowest setting. Line a large baking tray with nonstick baking paper. Remove the fruit from the pan with a slotted spoon (reserve the syrup) and place on the baking tray. Dry the fruit in the oven until dry to the touch.

4. Add the wine and honey to the syrup in the pan, and bring to a boil over a low heat. Boil for 5 minutes.

5. Warm the mustard seeds gently in another pan until they begin to pop. Stir the mustard seeds into the honey mixture, mixing well, and remove from the heat. Stir in the mustard.

6. Put the fruit into hot sterilized jars and pour over the syrup. Seal tightly, label, and leave to cool. Store in the refrigerator.

PICCALILLI

The recipe for "sweet Indian pickle" was brought to England in the 17th century and became known as piccalilli. Homemade piccalilli is much tastier and has a better texture than the commercial version. It is delicious with cold meats and cheeses. Use a mixture of cauliflower, cucumber, green beans, green tomatoes, pickling onions, and zucchini.

TOTAL TIME: 40 MINUTES, PLUS STANDING OVERNIGHT | MAKES: ABOUT TWO 32-OZ (1 L) JARS

- 3 lbs 5 oz (1.5 kg) prepared vegetables (see introduction)
- 6 oz (175 g) salt
- 8½ cups (2 L) water
- 4 oz (110 g) demerara sugar
- 1 tsp ground ginger
- 3¼ cups (750 mL) white distilled vinegar
- 1 oz (25 g) plain flour
- 2 tsp turmeric
- 1 Tbsp (8 g) mustard powder

1. Cut all the vegetables into small, even-sized pieces and place in a large bowl.
2. Dissolve the salt in the water and pour over the vegetables. Keep the vegetables submerged with a weighted plate and cover the bowl with a cloth.
3. Leave to stand for 24 hours. Drain the vegetables and rinse thoroughly.
4. Place the vegetables in a large, heavy-based pan with the sugar, ginger, and three-quarters of the vinegar. Bring to a boil.
5. Reduce the heat and simmer gently until as crisp or as tender as you like them. Crisp vegetables will need only 5 minutes simmering. Remove the vegetables with a slotted spoon, drain well, and put into hot sterilized jars.
6. Mix the flour, turmeric, and mustard powder with the remaining vinegar, and stir into the hot liquid in the pan. Bring to a boil and boil for about 1 minute until thick enough to coat the back of a wooden spoon, then remove from the heat and pour over the vegetables.
7. Gently bang the jars on a work surface to remove any air bubbles and top up with more sauce if necessary.
8. Cover and seal while hot and store for 3 months before using.

PICKLED CUCUMBERS

These crunchy cucumbers are perfect with meat and fish or placed in a burger.

TOTAL TIME: 30 MINUTES, PLUS 12 HOURS STANDING AND 2 WEEKS STORING
MAKES: ABOUT ONE 16-OZ (500 ML) JARS

- 1 lb (450 g) small cucumbers
- Sea salt, to taste
- 3 cups (700 mL) white wine vinegar
- 3 bay leaves
- 6 black peppercorns
- 6 coriander seeds
- 6 allspice berries
- 2 cloves garlic, chopped
- 4 sprigs dill leaves

1. Put the cucumbers in a shallow dish and cover with sea salt. Leave to stand overnight, then drain and rinse well. Pat dry.
2. Put the vinegar and spices in a pan and bring to a boil. Boil for 10 minutes, then remove from the heat and leave until cold.
3. Pack the cucumbers into cold sterilized glass jars, layering them with the garlic and dill.
4. Strain the cold vinegar mixture through a sieve over the cucumbers, making sure that the jars are filled.
5. Seal with vinegar-proof lids and label the jars and leave for 2 weeks before eating.

PICKLED KUMQUATS

These are delicious with ice cream, in a fruit salad, or dropped into cocktails.

TOTAL TIME: 50 MINUTES | MAKES: 25–30 PIECES

- 25–30 kumquats
- 2 cups (500 mL) water, plus more to cover
- 1 lb (450 g) sugar
- 1 vanilla pod, split

1. Put the kumquats into a large pan and add just enough water to cover the fruit.
2. Bring to a boil and when foam forms on the surface reduce the heat and boil gently for a further 10 minutes. Drain and set aside.
3. Pour the 2 cups (500 mL) water into a large pan and add the sugar. Heat gently, stirring until the sugar has dissolved.
4. Add the kumquats and vanilla pod and bring to a boil. Reduce the heat and simmer, stirring occasionally until the kumquats are transparent and soft. Discard the vanilla pod.
5. Spoon the kumquats and syrup into hot sterilized jars, cover and seal tightly. Label and leave to cool, then store in the refrigerator for up to 2 weeks.

PICKLED MUSHROOMS

Use small white mushrooms for this recipe. If you wish, you can use white wine vinegar instead of white malt vinegar. Mace enhances the flavor of the mushrooms. Leave these pickles for a few days before eating to allow the flavor to develop.

TOTAL TIME: 30 MINUTES | MAKES: ABOUT ONE 16-OZ (500 ML) JAR

- Water (see step 1)
- Pinch of salt
- 16 oz (450 g) button mushrooms, stalks removed
- 2½ cups (600 mL) white malt vinegar
- Whole cloves
- 10 peppercorns
- 2 blades of mace
- 1 Tbsp (18 g) salt

1. Put the mushrooms into a small pan, and just cover with water. Add salt and bring to a boil. Boil for 10 minutes, then remove from the heat and drain very well.

2. Put the vinegar, spices, and salt into a medium heavy-based pan, and bring to a boil. Simmer for 10 minutes, then remove from the heat and allow to cool completely. Put the cold mushrooms into jars and pour over the cold vinegar.

3. Cover, seal, and label.

PICKLED ONIONS

These crunchy pickled onions are a great favorite and are delicious with cheese, cold meats, and poultry, as well as in salads. If you like sweet pickled onions, add the sugar; otherwise, omit this. The spices add an aromatic flavor to the onions and vinegar.

TOTAL TIME: 40 MINUTES, PLUS STANDING OVERNIGHT | MAKES: ABOUT FIVE 8-OZ (250 ML) JARS

- 2 lbs 3 oz (1 kg) small pickling onions or shallots, peeled
- 25 g (1 oz) salt
- 32 oz (1 L) malt vinegar
- 1 tsp coriander seeds (optional)
- 1 tsp peppercorns (optional)
- 2 Tbsp (25 g) granulated or superfine sugar (optional)

1. Put the onions into a large bowl with the salt and mix together. Cover and leave overnight.
2. Rinse thoroughly in cold water and leave to dry on absorbent kitchen paper or on a clean tea towel for about 15 minutes. Pack the onions into cold, sterilized jars.
3. Put the vinegar, spices, and sugar (if using) into a medium pan, and slowly bring to a boil over a low heat until the sugar has dissolved completely. Cook steadily for 15 minutes, then remove from the heat and allow to cool completely.
4. Strain the vinegar through a sieve over the onions to cover completely. Cover and seal tightly. Store in a cool, dark cupboard for two weeks before eating.

PICKLED PLUMS

These piquant plums are delicious with cold pies as well as any cold meats and poultry. You can use small red plums, damsons, or greengages in this recipe, and each will give a slightly different result.

TOTAL TIME: 40 MINUTES | MAKES: ABOUT ONE 16-OZ (500 ML) JAR

- 1 lb (450 g) small plums, stalks removed
- 1¼ cups (300 mL) white distilled vinegar
- 8 oz (225 g) granulated or superfine sugar
- Finely pared rind of ½ lemon
- Small piece fresh root ginger, bruised
- 4 whole cloves, peeled
- 1 cinnamon stick

1. Prick the plums all over with a darning needle and place in a medium, heavy-based pan. Cover with vinegar and add the sugar.
2. Tie the lemon rind and spices in a piece of muslin and add to the pan.
3. Heat gently, stirring until the sugar has dissolved completely, then bring to a boil. Reduce the heat and simmer very gently until the fruit is tender, but don't let the skins break.
4. Remove the fruit with a slotted spoon and pack into warmed, sterilized jars.
5. Discard the muslin and boil the liquid rapidly for 5 minutes, then remove from the heat. Pour immediately over the plums to cover completely.
6. Cover and seal tightly.

PICKLED RED CABBAGE

This is one of the most popular pickles and is excellent with cheeses and cold meats. It is also delicious served as an accompaniment to meaty stews and sausages. It is best eaten within two to three months, before the cabbage begins to lose its crispness.

TOTAL TIME: 30 MINUTES, PLUS 24 HOURS STANDING AND COOLING TIME
MAKES: ABOUT FIVE 8-OZ (250 ML) JARS

- 2 firm red cabbages, cut into fine shreds across the grain
- 4 oz (110 g) salt
- 2½ cups (600 mL) red wine vinegar
- 2½ cups (600 mL) distilled malt vinegar
- 3 bay leaves
- 1 Tbsp (7 g) juniper berries (optional)

1. Put a layer of cabbage in a large bowl and sprinkle with salt. Repeat until all the cabbage has been used, ending with a layer of salt. Leave to stand for 24 hours, then drain off the liquid.

2. Rinse the cabbage well in cold water, then drain thoroughly.

3. Heat both vinegars in a large pan and bring to a boil. Reduce the heat and simmer for 5 minutes, then remove from the heat and allow to cool completely.

4. Pack the cabbage into cold, sterilized jars with the bay leaves and juniper berries if using. Pour in the cold vinegar to cover completely.

5. Cover, seal, and label. Allow to mature for a week before eating.

PICKLED WATERMELON RIND

A sweet-sour condiment that pairs well with any meat dish.

TOTAL TIME: 1 HOUR 20 MINUTES, PLUS STANDING OVERNIGHT | MAKES: ABOUT ONE 16-OZ (500 ML) JAR

- 2 lbs 3 oz (1 kg) watermelon rind
- 3 Tbsp (54 g) salt
- 5½ cups (1.3 L) water
- 2 lbs (900 g) sugar
- 2 cups (450 mL) white vinegar
- 6 cinnamon sticks
- 2 Tbsp (15 g) whole cloves
- 2 Tbsp (15 g) whole allspice

1. To prepare the rind, trim off the outer green skin and most of the pink flesh, leaving only a bit of pink on white rind. Cut the rind into 4" (10 cm) pieces.
2. Soak the rind overnight in a brine made of the salt and 3¾ cups (900 mL) water. In the morning, drain, cover with fresh water, and cook until tender.
3. Heat the sugar, vinegar, and remaining water in a pan to boiling point. Tie the cinnamon sticks, cloves, and allspice in a muslin bag and add to the pan. Add the cooked rind and simmer for about 45 minutes until the rind is transparent.
4. Pack the rind into hot sterilized jars.
5. Remove the spice bag from the syrup and bring to a boil again. Pour a boiling syrup over the rind, making sure the syrup completely covers the rind. Seal with vinegar-proof lids and label.

PRESERVED LEMONS

Finely chopped, these add a punchy kick to salad dressings for serving with fish. Sauté with garlic, olive oil, and leafy greens, or use in a traditional Moroccan tagine.

TOTAL TIME: 20 MINUTES, PLUS 30 DAYS STANDING | MAKES: 20 PIECES

- 5 lemons, quartered
- 3 Tbsp (55 g) sea salt
- 3 cloves
- ½ tsp fennel seeds
- 4 black peppercorns
- 1 bay leaf
- Lemon juice

1. Sprinkle salt on the exposed lemon flesh.
2. Place 1 tablespoon of salt in the bottom of a 16-oz (500 mL) jar. Pack in the lemons as tightly as possible, pushing them down, adding more salt and the spices between the layers. Tuck in the bay leaf.
3. Press the lemons down to release their juices and to make room for the remaining lemons. If the juice released from the squashed fruit does not cover them, add freshly squeezed lemon juice. Leave some air space at the top before sealing the jar.
4. Leave the lemons for 30 days in a warm place, shaking the jar from time to time to distribute the salt and juice. Rinse the lemons under running water before using.

SPICED PICKLED BLACKBERRIES

Here, whole blackberries are covered in a lightly spiced vinegar syrup and make a tasty and unusual accompaniment to cold meats, game, and cheese.

TOTAL TIME: 30 MINUTES | MAKES: ABOUT SEVEN 8-OZ (250 ML) JARS

- 1¼ cups (300 mL) red wine vinegar
- 1 lb (450 g) white or brown sugar
- ½ tsp ground cinnamon
- ½ tsp ground ginger
- ½ tsp ground cloves
- 53 oz (1.5 kg) blackberries

1. Put the vinegar, sugar, and spices into a large, heavy-based pan, and heat gently until the sugar has dissolved. Bring to a boil, reduce the heat, and simmer gently for a few minutes.

2. Add the blackberries and simmer for about 4–6 minutes until the blackberries are soft but still whole. Remove the berries with a slotted spoon, and pack into warmed, sterilized jars.

3. Boil the vinegar and sugar rapidly for about 5 minutes, or until the mixture forms a thick syrup. Remove from the heat, then pour the hot syrup into the jars of fruit to cover completely.

4. Cover and seal tightly. Leave for at least three weeks before using.

Spiced Pickled Pears

In the days when fruit was only available in season, it was often preserved in this way. These pears are a delicious accompaniment to any cold meats or poultry. You can use apples or quinces instead of pears if you like.

TOTAL TIME: 55 MINUTES | MAKES: ABOUT SEVEN 8-OZ (250 ML) JARS

- 3 lbs 5 oz (1.5 kg) cooking or hard pears
- Slightly salted cold water
- Dash of lemon juice
- 2½ cups (600 mL) white distilled vinegar
- 1 tsp pumpkin pie spice
- ½ tsp grated nutmeg
- 1 tsp ground cinnamon
- 1 lb (450 g) granulated or superfine sugar
- Finely pared rind of ½ lemon

1. Peel, halve (or quarter), and core the pears, and put into a bowl of slightly salted water with lemon juice, to prevent them becoming brown.

2. Mix a little of the vinegar with the spices. Put the remaining vinegar and the sugar into a pan with the lemon rind. Heat gently until the sugar has dissolved completely, add the spice mixture, then bring to a boil.

3. Rinse the pears and add to the pan. Simmer gently for about 15–20 minutes until the pears look clear and are tender but not broken. Remove the pears with a slotted spoon and put into warmed, sterilized jars.

4. Discard the lemon peel and boil the liquid in the pan rapidly for about 10–15 minutes until it has thickened to a syrup.

5. Remove from the heat. Pour over the pears to cover them completely and seal the jars immediately.

TANGY PICKLED ONIONS

Spicy, tangy onions make an unusual accompaniment to all sorts of foods.

TOTAL TIME: 30 MINUTES, PLUS STANDING OVERNIGHT | MAKES: ABOUT THREE 8-OZ (250 ML) JARS

- 1 cup (300 g) pickling onions
- Sea salt for sprinkling
- 1½ cups (350 mL) white wine vinegar
- 2 tsp salt
- ½ tsp dried chili flakes
- 1 cinnamon stick
- 2 star anise pods
- ½ Tbsp (3 g) grated fresh ginger
- ½ Tbsp (7 mL) soy sauce
- 4 oz (120 g) sugar
- 2 Tbsp (30 mL) sherry
- 3 cloves per jar

1. Put the onions in a large bowl and pour over a kettle of boiling water. Leave for 20 seconds then pour into a colander, return to the bowl, and pour over lots of very cold water. The skins should now peel off very easily.

2. Put a layer of onions on the base of a large bowl and then sprinkle liberally with salt; add another layer of onions and sprinkle liberally with salt. Repeat the process until all the onions are in the bowl and have been salted.

3. Leave overnight and then rinse well and allow them to dry.

4. Mix the vinegar, salt, spices, soy sauce, sugar, and sherry in a pan and bring to a boil for 30 seconds, then remove from the heat.

5. Drop the cloves into hot sterilized jars and add the onions until the jars are full.

6. Pour the hot vinegar mixture through a sieve over the onions. Cover, seal with vinegar-proof lids and label and leave for about 2 weeks before eating.

Bottling

We have Napoleon Bonaparte to thank for the idea of bottling fruit. In 1800, he offered a prize of 12,000 francs to anyone who could create a method of preserving food as a means of providing his armies with daily rations. The winner was Nicolas Appert, who put forward his invention of bottling. Bottling fruit has remained steadfastly popular throughout the years and is a marvelous way to preserve a surplus of fruit.

Preserving through bottling lets us enjoy seasonal produce year-round.

Jars should be boiled before use.

Equipment

Use proper preserving jars with matching lids and close fitting rubber rings and wide necks so the fruits can be packed in easily. These are available from kitchen shops and come in varying sizes so you can bottle large or small quantities. Chipped jars or cracked lids must not be used as the seal will be poor and the contents could be become contaminated.

Kilner or Mason jars are ideal for storing homemade preserves and come in a range of sizes. A Kilner jar is a glass jar that has a lid in two sections to ensure an airtight seal. A metal disc sits on top of the jar, and it is secured in place with a metal screw band containing a rubber seal. Another widely available glass jar has a rubber seal and a metal hinge, which forms an airtight seal when closed.

Jars and lids must be well washed, well rinsed, and put into a large pan of cold water. Bring slowly to a boil, then remove from the heat and leave the jars in the water until needed. Don't wipe the jars, just shake off any surplus water.

A sugar or preserving thermometer is advisable, to ensure the correct temperature has been reached.

Ingredients

Fruit must be sound, unbruised, unblemished and just ripe. Rinse the fruit gently under cold running water. Very fragile fruits, such as raspberries, only require a gentle swirl around in a bowl of cold water, then draining on absorbent kitchen paper. Then prepare the fruit as directed in the recipe.

Tomatoes are popular for bottling and there are hundreds of varieties available today—green, orange, yellow, red, tiny, huge, round or plum shaped. Tomatoes hate the cold so are best stored at room temperature. If you do have some in the refrigerator, take them out a few hours before you plan to use them.

Preparation

The fruit is packed into jars as tightly as possible without damaging it. The jars are then filled with cold water or syrup, and then the rubber rings, lids, and screw bands are put into place. Give the bands a half turn to loosen them slightly (the glass expands during sterilization). If using bottling jars with clips instead of screw bands, move the clips slightly to the side of the lids to decrease the pressure to the jars.

Line a deep, heavy pan with a thick layer of paper or cloth to prevent the jars cracking. Put the jars in the pan, making sure they don't touch each other, and pour in cold water to come right up to the neck of the jars. Cover with a lid or triple thickness of foil.

Insert jars of fruit (covered) into a large pan and fill with water for the bottling process.

Very slowly bring the water to simmering point—this should take at least 1½ hours. Follow the directions in individual recipes, as some fruits will be required to reach a higher temperature than others. Check by using a preserving thermometer. Do not try to hurry this process; if the water is heated too quickly, the fruit may rise in the bottles and more time may be needed at the maximum temperature for the heat to penetrate the fruit in the center of the jars.

The temperature must be maintained for 30 minutes. Remove the pan from the heat, then carefully remove the hot jars from the pan. Wear thick oven gloves to do this. Stand the hot jars on a wooden chopping board—not a cold surface or the jars may crack. Tighten the screw bands or move the clips to the center of the lids, and leave to stand for 24 hours.

When cool, remove the screw bands or clips, and test that the lids are tightly sealed. This is to ensure that a complete vacuum has been formed during the processing and that no air is in the jars. If not, the fruit is not safe to keep and should be eaten the same day.

...matoes are popular for bottling and ...re best stored at room temperature.

Store bottled fruits in a cool, dark, dry cupboard. Check the seals from time to time to ensure the jars are still tightly sealed. Once opened, store in the refrigerator.

Safety Note: Only fruits and tomatoes should be bottled. Vegetables must not be bottled, as the results could prove fatal if the correct temperature is not reached.

BOTTLING INDIVIDUAL FRUITS

- **Apples:** Peel, core and slice. They will need 15 minutes at 180°F (82°C).
- **Apricots:** Leave whole. They will need 15 minutes at 180°F (82°C).
- **Blackberries:** Leave whole. They will need 10 minutes at 165°F (74°C).
- **Cherries:** Remove stalks but leave whole. They will need 15 minutes at 180°F (82°C).
- **Damsons:** Remove stalks but leave whole. They will need 15 minutes at 180°F (82°C).
- **Gooseberries:** Top and tail but leave whole. They will need 15 minutes at 180°F (82°C).
- **Mulberries:** Leave whole. They will need 10 minutes at 165°F (74°C).
- **Peaches:** Blanch in boiling water for 1 minute and remove the skins. Cut in half and remove pits. They will need 15 minutes at 180°F (82°C).
- **Pears:** Use dessert pears only. Cut in half or quarters and scoop out the soft cores. They will need 30 minutes at 190°F (88°C).
- **Plums:** Remove stalks but leave whole or cut in half and remove pits. They will need 15 minutes at 180°F (82°C).
- **Raspberries:** Leave whole. They will need 10 minutes at 165°F (74°C).

WHAT CAN GO WRONG?

- **Fruit may shrink** during storage. This is due to air in the jars.
- **Air bubbles**. After putting the fruit into the jars, tap the jars to remove any air bubbles.
- **Moldy fruits** are caused by storing the jars in moist, warm conditions.
- **Discolored fruit** is caused by storing the jars incorrectly.
- **Light** will bleach their color.

Wear a thick rubber glove when removing the jars, because the water will be boiling.

APPLES AND OTHER HARD FRUITS

Fruits that become brown when exposed to air should be dropped into a bowl of water with a little lemon juice added to prevent this happening.

TOTAL TIME: 2 HOURS, PLUS 24 HOURS STANDING
MAKES: ABOUT 32 OZ (1 L) PER 2 LBS 10 OZ (1.2 KG) FRUIT

- ⅔ cup (150 mL) syrup for every 1 lb (450 g) fruit
- 8 oz (225 g) granulated or superfine sugar for every 2½ cups (600 mL) water

1. To make the syrup, heat the sugar and water in a medium-large pan (depending on the amount of sugar and water used). Slowly bring to a boil for about 2 minutes until the sugar has dissolved completely. Remove from the heat and allow to cool completely.

2. Pack the fruit into the prepared jars and pour in the cold syrup. This is best done slowly to allow the syrup to seep to the bottom of the jars.

3. Fit on the lids as directed on page 119. Line a deep, heavy pan with a thick layer of paper or cloth. Put the jars in the pan, not touching, and pour in cold water right up to the neck of the jars. Cover with a lid or triple thickness of foil.

4. Very slowly bring the water to simmering point—at least 1½ hours. Follow the directions for individual fruits (page 120), as some will require a longer time than others. Check by using a preserving thermometer. The temperature must be maintained for the stated time.

5. Remove the pan from the heat. Remove the hot jars from the pan. Wear thick oven gloves to do this. Stand the hot jars on a wooden chopping board—not a cold surface.

6. Tighten the screw bands or move the clips to the center of the lids and leave to stand for 24 hours.

7. Remove the screw bands or clips and test that the lids are tightly sealed. If not, the fruit is not safe to keep and should be eaten the same day.

BOTTLED TOMATOES

Medium or large tomatoes should have skins removed after being blanched in boiling water.

TOTAL TIME: 2 HOURS 15 MINUTES, PLUS 24 HOURS STANDING

MAKES: ABOUT SEVEN 8-OZ (250 ML) JARS

- 3 lbs 5 oz (1.5 kg) tomatoes
- 1½ Tbsp (22.5 mL) lemon juice
- 1½ tsp salt
- 1½ tsp sugar

1. If using small tomatoes, remove the stalks but leave whole. Medium or large tomatoes can be blanched in boiling water to remove the skins, then cut into halves or quarters.
2. Toss the tomatoes in the lmon juice, sugar, and salt. Pack tightly into jars with no air spaces between them.
3. Put the jars in a large pan, making sure they don't touch each other, and pour in cold water up to the neck of the jars. Cover with a lid or triple thickness of foil. Very slowly bring the water to simmering point—at least 1½ hours.
4. Whole tomatoes will need 30 minutes at 190°F (88°C). Halved or quartered tomatoes will need 40 minutes at the same temperature. Check by using a preserving thermometer. The temperature must be maintained for the stated time.
5. Remove the pan from the heat and carefully remove the hot jars from the pan. Wear thick oven gloves to do this. Stand the hot jars on a wooden chopping board—not a cold surface. Tighten the screw bands or move the clips to the center of the lids and leave to stand for 24 hours.
6. Remove the screw bands or clips and test that the lids are tightly sealed. If they are not, the tomatoes are not safe to keep and should be eaten the same day.

FRUIT SALAD

The fruit in this recipe is bottled by a different method. The fruit is packed into hot jars, covered with boiling syrup, and placed in a low oven to sterilize the fruit. The success with this method rests in the quick filling and sealing of the bottles as soon as they are removed from the oven.

TOTAL TIME: 1 HOUR 45 MINUTES, PLUS 24 HOURS STANDING

MAKES: FOUR 32-OZ (1 L) JARS

- 1 lb (450 g) granulated or superfine sugar
- 4½ cups (1.1 L) water
- 2 lbs 3 oz (1 kg) Victoria plums, cut in half and pits removed
- 8 oz (225 g) seedless grapes
- 6 peaches, skinned, cut in half, and pits removed
- 4 dessert pears, cut in quarters and cores removed

1. Put the sugar and water into a medium pan over a low heat, and stir until the sugar has dissolved completely. Bring to a boil and boil for 2 minutes. Preheat the oven to 300°F (150°C/gas 2).

2. Pack an equal quantity of fruit into hot, sterilized jars. Pour a boiling syrup over the fruit to within 1" (2.5 cm) of the top of the jars. Arrange the jars about 2" (5 cm) apart on baking trays lined with newspaper. Cover the jars with lids (but not screw bands) and place in the oven for 1½ hours.

3. Remove from the oven and screw the caps on tightly to seal. Leave to stand for 24 hours.

4. Remove the screw bands or clips and test that the lids are tightly sealed. If not, the fruit is not safe to keep and should be eaten the same day.

Salting

Salting green beans and white cabbage is a time-honored way of preserving summer and autumn vegetables to use during the winter months. Salt is an excellent preservative, and salted vegetables will keep for about six months.

Make sure to use dry produce when salting for storage.

Sea salt and pickling salt are best for preservation.

Equipment

Large stone or glass jars are necessary to layer the vegetables with the salt. These must be scrupulously clean and dry.

Ingredients

Vegetables used for salting must be fresh, young, tender, unblemished, and completely dry.

Salt has two effects: it draws water from the vegetables by the process of osmosis. Then the salt in the resultant brine sets off the fermentation process of the lactic bacteria. The ensuing fermentation is bacteriologically complex and produces a diverse range of multifaceted flavors. In Europe, the most common salted vegetable is white cabbage, which when salted and fermented, is known as sauerkraut.

Salt inhibits attack by harmful microorganisms. Sea salt or special pickling salt are the best types to use as they are free from impurities and come in the form of crystals. Table salt is mass produced and refined and has been treated to ensure it pours easily.

Spices such as juniper berries and caraway seeds are often used to flavor sauerkraut. Caraway has a warm, pungent aroma and sweet tangy flavor. Juniper berries add a slightly resinous note of pine to the flavor.

Preparation

The vegetables are prepared according to type (runner beans and French beans are the most usual) and will be indicated in the recipes. Use only fresh, young, tender beans; wash them and dry thoroughly. The vegetables are then packed down well into the jars, alternating with layers of salt sprinkled generously over them. Begin and end with a thick layer of salt and press down the vegetables as you layer them. Most bacteria cannot survive in a highly salty environment, and this is how the food is preserved.

Cover and leave in a cool, dark place for four days. The vegetables will have shrunk, so it is necessary to top up the jars with more vegetables and salt, finishing with a layer of salt. As the salt draws liquid from the vegetables, it will form a strong brine. The brine should be kept intact, otherwise air pockets will form and the vegetables will deteriorate rapidly, and bacteria and mold will develop.

The jars are sealed tightly and stored in a cupboard for up to six months. Don't place the jars on stone or brick, as moisture will be drawn out of them.

Before eating the vegetables, it is essential to rinse them thoroughly in cold water and then soak them in warm water for two hours. Cook for about 20–30 minutes or until tender. Drain and serve as for fresh vegetables.

WHAT CAN GO WRONG?

There's not really anything that can go wrong when salting vegetables. Just remember to rinse them very well before eating or they will be overpoweringly salty.

Pack layers of cabbage and salt to make sauerkraut.

FRENCH BEANS

French beans, also called string beans, are smaller and rounder than runner beans and have a mild but very pleasant flavor. They originated in Central and South America and were introduced into Europe in the 16th century.

TOTAL TIME: 20 MINUTES, PLUS 4 DAYS STANDING | MAKES: ABOUT ONE 16-OZ (500 ML) JAR

1. Follow the recipe and method as with Runner Beans (page 133) but leave the beans whole.
2. To serve, rinse thoroughly and cook in simmering water for about 10 minutes, or until tender.

RUNNER BEANS

Runner beans are also known as scarlet runner beans due to their attractive, vivid red flowers, which is originally the reason they were grown in gardens. Young, fresh runner beans are one of the best summer vegetables, succulently tender and packed with flavor. Tiny young beans are very tender and don't need topping, tailing, or stringing.

TOTAL TIME: 25 MINUTES, PLUS 4 DAYS STANDING | MAKES: ABOUT ONE 16-OZ (500 ML) JAR

- 3 lbs 5 oz (1.5 kg) fresh young runner beans, topped and tailed
- 1 lb (450 g) coarse or sea salt, not table salt

1. Remove any strings from the sides of the beans if necessary, and cut the beans into thin diagonal slices.
2. Put a thick layer of salt in the base of large glass jars or earthenware crock. Add a layer of beans. Repeat until all the beans have been used, ending in a layer of salt. Press each layer of beans down well as you layer them. When the jar is full cover with a lid.
3. Leave in a cool dark place for 4 days, by which time the beans will have shrunk. Top up the jars with more beans and salt, finishing with a layer of salt.
4. Seal tightly and store for up to 6 months.
5. To serve, rinse thoroughly and cook in simmering water for about 10 minutes, or until tender.

SAUERKRAUT

The cabbage ferments as it is stored and has a unique and distinctive sour flavor. Homemade sauerkraut is much tastier than the commercial variety and is well worth the time and effort it takes to make. Caraway, bay leaves, and juniper berries add an aromatic flavor, but you can omit these if you wish. It is worth making a large amount as it is a lengthy process.

TOTAL TIME: 35 MINUTES, PLUS 2 WEEKS STANDING | MAKES: ABOUT SEVEN 32-OZ (1 L) JARS

- 4 large heads white cabbage (about 11 lbs [5 kg]), finely shredded
- 5 oz (150 g) sea salt
- Few juniper berries (optional)
- Few caraway seeds (optional)
- Few bay leaves (optional)

1. Mix the cabbage and salt in a very large mixing bowl. Pack tightly into a clean wooden tub or 9 L stoneware jar, adding a few juniper berries, caraway seeds, and bay leaves (if using).
2. Cover the top of the cabbage with a clean cloth or double thickness of muslin. Add a stopper that fits inside the container or put a plate on top that fits inside the jar or tub.
3. Stand a heavy weight (a stone or brick is ideal) on the plate, and leave in a warm room 70°F (21°C) for 4–5 days. When froth appears, remove the weight and plate and skim it off. Leave to stand for another 2 days and skim off the froth again. Repeat this process for 2 weeks.
4. The sauerkraut is now ready to eat and can be kept in the refrigerator for several weeks or frozen.
5. To serve, rinse the salty juices out before using. Taste a little, and if it is still too salty, soak it for about 20 minutes in tepid water, then rinse again. Drain and squeeze out the liquid. Sauerkraut can be eaten as it is or cooked by simmering in a pan of boiling water for about 15–30 minutes until done to your liking. You can also cook sauerkraut by stewing it very slowly for about 2 hours in a pan with just enough water to cover. Alternatively, fry sauerkraut briefly in a little oil in a frying pan, then cover with boiling water and cook until done to your liking.

LONG-TERM STORAGE

- Drain off the brine into a large pan and add the cabbage. Heat to simmering point, and immediately put into warmed preserving jars.
- Line a deep heavy-based pan with a thick layer of paper or cloth to prevent the jars cracking. Put the jars in the pan, making sure they don't touch each other, and pour in cold water to come right up to the neck of the jars. Cover with a lid or triple thickness of foil. Very slowly bring the water to simmering point and simmer for 30 minutes.

- Carefully remove the jars from the pan. Wear thick oven gloves to do this. Stand the hot jars on a wooden chopping board—not a cold surface or the jars may crack. Tighten the screw bands or move the clips to the center of the lids and leave to stand for 24 hours. Remove the screw bands or clips and test that the lids are tightly sealed.
- Store the jars in a cool, dark place for up to a year.

Drying Fruits and Vegetables

Drying is one of the oldest methods of preserving. It removes the water from fruits and vegetables, and so deactivates the harmful microbes that cause spoiling, so the foods are preserved for a long time. Drying foods also concentrates their flavor. Use top-quality fruits and vegetables that are unblemished. The moisture content of each item and the thickness of the slices will affect drying time, so these timings are only approximate.

Drying has a lot of benefits
for produce.

Orange slices drying on parchment paper in the oven.

Equipment

It's easy to dry fruits and vegetables using an oven. You don't need any special equipment—just flat baking trays and airtight jars.

Popular Fruits and Vegetables for Drying

Almost any fruit can be dried. The most popular are apples, pears, and bananas. Popular vegetables for drying are green beans and mushrooms.

It's easy to dry fruits and vegetables using the oven.

Preparation

Reject any damaged fruits or vegetables, e.g., bruising, discoloration, or evidence of mold. Keep pieces the same size so that they dry at the same rate. Lay the fruit on the baking trays so that it does not overlap.

Dried apples make for a great snack!

APPLES AND PEARS

1. Preheat the oven to 212°F (100°C). Place two wire racks over two baking trays.
2. Peel the apples (optional), core them, and slice into ¼" (6 mm) rings.
3. Stir 2 Tbsp (30 mL) lemon juice into a large bowl of water, and add the apples to prevent them from browning.
4. Pat the apples dry and place on the wire racks.
5. Put in the oven for 2–4 hours until the apples feel flexible and dry. Store in an airtight jar for up to 3 months.

APRICOTS, PEACHES, AND PLUMS

1. Cut the fruit in half and remove the pits. Lay cut side up on wire racks over baking trays as above.
2. Sprinkle with lemon juice and dry in the oven as above.

BANANAS

1. Set the oven to its lowest setting, about 250°F (120°C).
2. Peel firm, ripe bananas, and cut in half lengthwise. Cut each length into slices and place on racks, cut side up as for apples.
3. Put in the oven for at least 6 hours, turning them over halfway through.
4. Leave to cool and store as for apples.

FRENCH AND RUNNER BEANS

1. Set the oven to its lowest setting, about 250°F (120°C).
2. Top and tail the beans. Leave young beans whole, but cut older beans into thin strips.
3. Blanch in boiling water for 3 minutes, then drain well. Place on racks as for apples.
4. Put in the oven for 2–3 hours until crisp. Store as for apples.

MUSHROOMS

1. Set the oven to its lowest setting, about 250°F (120°C).
2. Thinly slice the mushrooms and place on wire racks as for apples. Place in the oven, leaving the oven door slightly open to allow the moisture to escape.
3. Leave for 2–5 hours until dry and store as for apples.

PEPPERS

1. Set the oven to its lowest setting, about 250°F (120°C).
2. Cut the peppers into thin strips, discarding the cores, seeds, and stems.
3. Place on the racks and put into the oven with the oven door slightly ajar. Leave to dry for at least 12 hours.
4. Leave to cool and store as for apples.

TOMATOES

1. Set the oven to its lowest setting, about 250°F (120°C).
2. Cut the tomatoes in half, and place them face up on wire racks. Sprinkle with a little salt, and brush lightly with olive oil.
3. Put in the oven for 6–12 hours, depending on size.
4. Pack into warm sterilized jars and cover with warm olive oil. Seal and store for up to 6 months.

Preserves as Gifts

Delicious homemade goodies make delightful presents for Christmas or any time of year. They are well worth the time and effort involved, as they're made and given with love and are very much appreciated. Although, nowadays, virtually everything is available ready-made, it's so much better to offer something unique that will be far more delicious than its commercially mass-produced equivalent.

All these delicious recipes can be prepared well ahead, and they cost less to make at home too. These tempting recipes are also ideal to give as presents and perfect for donating to Christmas markets and bazaars. Use decorative jars and tie with a pretty ribbon for a festive look. Scraps of bright material or lace can be cut to cover jar lids. Make gift tags from stiff cardstock, cut into seasonal shapes. Use a silver or gold marker or pens to give a festive look. Add tinsel, glitter, or sequins for a touch of Christmas sparkle.

A homemade gift comes from the heart, perfect for the holiday season.

CRANBERRY CHUTNEY

A lovely, festive chutney to serve with meat, poultry, or cheese.

TOTAL TIME: 1 HOUR | MAKES: ABOUT ONE 16-OZ (500 ML) JAR

- 1 lb (450 g) cooking apples (peeled and cored weight), roughly chopped
- 1 lb (450 g) cranberries
- 1 onion, finely chopped
- 1 tsp allspice berries
- 1 tsp cardamom seeds
- 1 tsp pumpkin pie spice
- 1¼ cups (300 mL) cider vinegar
- 12 oz (350 g) sugar
- Salt and pepper, to taste

1. Put the apples, cranberries, and onions into a large, heavy-based pan.
2. Tie the whole spices in muslin, and put into the pan with the pumpkin pie spice and vinegar. Cover the pan tightly and cook gently for 15 minutes.
3. Stir well and simmer, uncovered, until the fruit is soft. Add the sugar and stir until dissolved.
4. Cook steadily until the chutney is thick. Season to taste with salt and pepper. Remove the muslin bag.
5. Spoon into hot, sterilized jars. Cover with vinegar-proof lids, seal, and label.

MARRONS GLACÉS (CRYSTALLIZED CHESTNUTS)

Moist and succulently sweet, marrons glacés are one of France's favorite confections. They're expensive to buy but are not difficult to make at home, making an ideal Christmas gift when packed into attractive boxes.

TOTAL TIME: 3 HOURS, PLUS 36 HOURS STANDING | MAKES: 20–30 PIECES

- 1.1 lbs (500 g) chestnuts
- Boiling water (see step 2)
- 10½ oz (300 g) superfine or fine granulated sugar
- 1¼ cups (300 mL) water

1. With a sharp knife, make a couple of nicks across the pointed end of each chestnut.
2. Put into a pan and pour over boiling water. Heat for 4 minutes, drain, and peel while still warm.
3. Place the sugar and water in a pan, heat gently until the sugar has dissolved completely, then bring to a boil.
4. Simmer for 10 minutes, then add the chestnuts and simmer for 8 minutes. Remove from the heat, cover, and leave to stand overnight.
5. The next day, bring back to a boil and cook for 1 minute, then leave to cool.
6. Repeat a boiling and cooling process 3 times over the next 2 days until all the syrup is absorbed.
7. Heat the oven to 158°F (70°C). Line a large baking tray with nonstick baking paper.
8. Place the chestnuts on the tray and put into the oven, leaving the oven door slightly open. Leave for at least 2 hours until firm.
9. Wrap carefully in greaseproof paper when completely cold.

SPICED ORANGE SLICES

These are expensive to buy in food stores but are not difficult to make at home. They make a delicious accompaniment to ham, roast duck, or pork.

TOTAL TIME: 2 HOURS 20 MINUTES. | MAKES: ABOUT THREE 16-OZ (500 ML) JARS

- 6 unwaxed oranges
- Water (see step 2)
- 1¼ cups (300 mL) white wine vinegar
- 1 lb (450 g) granulated sugar
- 4 cloves
- 2 cinnamon sticks
- 1 star anise

1. Cut the fruit into ¼" (6 mm) slices and discard the seeds.
2. Put the orange slices into a pan and pour over just enough cold water to cover. Bring to a boil, then reduce the heat, and simmer gently for about 1 hour until the peel is tender.
3. Remove the oranges with a slotted spoon to a bowl. Discard the water.
4. Put the vinegar, sugar, and spices into a pan and heat gently until the sugar has dissolved completely.
5. Bring to a boil and add the orange slices. Then reduce the heat and simmer gently for about 30–40 minutes until the orange slices are translucent. Remove from the heat.
6. Using a slotted spoon, put the oranges and cloves into warm, sterilized jars.
7. Return the pan to the heat and boil rapidly for 10 minutes to reduce the liquid and concentrate the flavor.
8. Pour over the fruit in the jars—there should be enough to cover the orange slices. Cover tightly with vinegar-proof lids and label.

SPICED PRUNES

These are delicious served with meat and poultry, but also with ice cream as a dessert.

TOTAL TIME: 25 MINUTES, PLUS 15 MINUTES STANDING | MAKES: ABOUT FOUR 16-OZ (500 ML) JARS

- 2 lbs (900 g) prunes, pitted
- Boiling water (see step 1)
- 2 cups (570 mL) red wine vinegar
- 8 oz (225 g) dark muscovado sugar
- 3 cinnamon sticks
- 2 blades mace
- 5 cloves
- 1 vanilla pod, split
- 3–5 Tbsp (44–74 mL) brandy

1. Place the prunes in a bowl and cover with boiling water. Stand for 15 minutes, then drain.
2. Put the vinegar, sugar, spices, and vanilla pod into a pan over a low heat and slowly bring to a boil. Simmer for 15 minutes. Remove the vanilla pod.
3. Pack the prunes into hot, sterilized jars (filling them as full as possible). Carefully pour the liquid over the prunes, making sure they are completely covered.
4. Spoon a tablespoon of brandy into each jar, then cover and seal tightly with vinegar-proof lids.

TRADITIONAL MINCEMEAT

Mincemeat, originally made with minced or shredded meat, dried fruits, and spices, was first recorded in 16th century England. Gradually, the meat was omitted, and today, the only remnant of meat in the recipe is the suet. There are also vegetarian mincemeats made with vegetable suet or no suet at all. Homemade mincemeat tastes much nicer than store bought and is easy to make. Make it one to three months before using, and keep in a cool, dry, dark place to mature.

TOTAL TIME: 25 MINUTES, PLUS 6 HOURS STANDING | MAKES: ABOUT THREE 16-OZ (500 ML) JARS

- 1 large cooking apple, grated
- 8 oz (225 g) sultanas
- 8 oz (225 g) currants
- 8 oz (225 g) raisins
- 2 oz (55 g) candied orange peel, finely chopped
- 2 oz (55 g) candied lemon peel, finely chopped
- 8 oz (225 g) shredded suet
- 2 oz (55 g) slivered almonds (optional)
- Zest and juice of 1 lemon
- Zest and juice of 1 orange
- 9 oz (250 g) dark brown muscovado sugar
- 2½ tsp (20 g) pumpkin pie spice
- ½ tsp grated nutmeg
- ½ tsp ground cinnamon
- ½ tsp ground ginger
- 7 Tbsp (100 mL) brandy

1. Mix all the ingredients together, except the brandy, in a large bowl. Stir well until thoroughly mixed.
2. Place the mixture in a large pan and heat gently until the suet and sugar have melted.
3. Remove from the heat, stir well, cover, and leave to cool completely until cold.
4. Stir in the brandy until well combined.
5. Pack into cold, sterilized jars, pressing down the mixture to ensure there are no air bubbles. Cover with wax discs, seal with lids, and label.

Uncooked Apple and Cranberry Mincemeat

For those who dislike the taste of traditional mincemeat, this recipe is for you. You can use hazelnuts or walnuts instead of almonds if you wish.

TOTAL TIME: 25 MINUTES, PLUS OVERNIGHT STANDING | MAKES: ABOUT SEVEN 8-OZ (250 ML) JARS

- 8 oz (227 g) shredded suet
- 8 oz (227 g) dried apricots, chopped
- 8 oz (227 g) cooking apples, peeled, cored, and chopped
- 3.8 oz (110 g) prunes, chopped
- 3.8 oz (110 g) dried cranberries
- 8 oz (227 g) sultanas
- 3.8 oz (110 g) glace cherries, chopped
- 3.8 oz (110 g) candied peel, finely diced
- 2 oz (55 g) blanched almonds, chopped
- 1 Tbsp (15 mL) clear honey
- 1 tsp ground cinnamon
- Large pinch of ground cloves
- Zest and juice of 1 lemon
- Zest and juice of 1 orange
- 2½ cups (600 mL) cider

1. Combine all the ingredients in a large mixing bowl, stirring very well.
2. Cover and leave to stand overnight to allow the flavors to blend.
3. Pack into cold sterilized jars, pressing down, making sure there are no air bubbles. Cover with waxed discs, seal with tight-fitting lids, and label.

Seasonal Produce
AUTUMN

VEGETABLES AND HERBS

Artichoke (globe and Jerusalem)	Celery	Parsnip	Squash
Bean (kidney and runner)	Cucumber	Potatoe	Sweetcorn
Broccoli	Leek	Pumpkin	Tomato
Cabbage	Lettuce	Radish	Turnip
Carrot	Mint	Rutabaga	Watercress
	Mushroom	Shallot	Zucchini
	Parsley	Spinach	

FRUITS

Apple (including crabapple)	Elderberry
Blackberry	Pear
Damson	Plum
	Raspberry

The zucchini is a member of the squash family.

Elderberries are fragrant like their flowers.

WINTER

VEGETABLES AND HERBS

Artichoke (globe and Jerusalem)	Carrot	Kale	Potato
	Cauliflower	Leek	Rutabaga
Beetroot	Celery root	Mushroom	Shallots
Brussels sprout	Celery	Onion	Turnip
Cabbage	Chicory	Parsnip	Watercress

FRUITS

Apple	Quince
Pear	

The rutabaga is the hybrid of a wild cabbage and turnip.

Pears have a mild flavor that can meld with many flavors in a jam.

SPRING

VEGETABLES AND HERBS

Artichoke (globe and Jerusalem)	Carrot	Mint	Spinach
Asparagus	Cauliflower	Mushroom	Spring green cabbage
Beetroot	Celery	New potato	Spring onion
Broccoli	Cucumber	Parsley	Watercress
	Lettuce	Rutabaga	

FRUITS

Apple   Rhubarb

Use mild mint leaves for preserves.   **Only eat the stems on a rhubarb.**

SUMMER

VEGETABLES AND HERBS

Artichoke (globe and Jerusalem)	Cabbage	Lettuce	Radish
	Carrot	Mint	Spinach
Basil	Cauliflower	Mushroom	Tomato
Bean (broad, kidney, and runner)	Celery	Parsley	Watercress
	Cucumber	Pea	Zucchini

FRUITS

Blackcurrant	Pear
Cherry	Plum
Damson	Raspberry
Gooseberry	Redcurrant
Greengage	Strawberry
Mulberry	

Scarlet runner beans are so named for their beautiful color.

Gooseberries taste differently depending on their color.

Photo Credits

Index

About the Author

Carol Wilson is a food writer, cookery consultant, and member of the Guild of Food Writers. She writes for a number of food publications both in the UK and the US and has written several cookbooks. Carol has also appeared on several TV food programs.